FELICIA CARTRIGHT

AND THE
PINK POODLE

Felicia

Joan

FELICIA CARTRIGHT

AND THE
PINK POODLE

BERNARD PALMER

ANEKO
PRESS

Cover Artwork: Adobe Firefly & Ideogram

Editor: Charlene Miskimen

Aneko Press *Youth*

www.anekopress.com

Aneko Press, Life Sentence Publishing, and our logos are trademarks of
Life Sentence Publishing, Inc.
203 E. Birch Street
P.O. Box 652
Abbotsford, WI 54405

JUVENILE FICTION / Religious / Christian / Action & Adventure

Paperback ISBN: 979-8-88936-318-7

eBook ISBN: 979-8-88936-319-4

10 9 8 7 6 5 4 3 2 1

Available where books are sold

CONTENTS

CHAPTER 1

A FASCINATING STORY

Felicia Cartright braked to a stop at the red sign, then swung Joan Bailey's gleaming, canary-yellow sports car out onto the highway and headed back to the formidable buildings of the Wellington School for Girls.

"I wish Joan could have been with us this evening, Shirley, but she had to cram for a make-up test in English on Monday morning and didn't think she could spare the time."

"I know. She came in and talked with me about it this morning." She paused, then added, "Tell me, has she *always* had trouble with her studies?"

"For as long as I've known her," Felicia answered. "It isn't that she can't get good grades. It's just that she usually has so many things going she doesn't take enough time to study."

Shirley brushed her long, soft brown hair back

from the delicate oval of her face with an uncertain gesture. For several minutes, she stared blankly at the dark highway ahead.

"I used to be the same way," she said. "In fact, I've been having plenty of trouble getting back in the study groove myself after being out of it for so long."

Felicia glanced at the slight, attractive figure of her companion as she stopped for a red light.

"That was a tremendous talk you gave this evening, Shirley."

The other girl's hazel eyes and smile were bright in contrast to the serious tenor of the meeting they had just left. There was a courageous set to her jaw and the thin line of her mouth, a quiet resourcefulness that Felicia had seen and admired from the first time she met her a little more than a month before. It was difficult to believe that she had been caught in the dreaded snare of drugs.

"Thank you, Felicia. I tried to give them something to think about."

"You did that. Make no mistake about it." Felicia could still see the shock in the eyes of the boys and girls as Shirley traced her progression from marijuana to speed and the amphetamines and finally to heroin. Shock had turned to horror as she described the agonies of withdrawal from heroin addiction and the fight back.

The lines in Shirley's face deepened. "If they'll only understand that it's for their own good," she murmured, "and that I only want to help them avoid the terrible things I went through."

"I'm sure you made them understand."

"I'm afraid there are some of them who are just the way I was a few years ago. People tried to tell me that weed could be harmful and that it led to stronger and even more potent drugs, but I didn't pay any attention. I knew better than anyone else." For the first time, bitterness stole into her voice. "And now, look at me!"

"You're getting along all right now, aren't you?"

"I guess so." She managed a thin breath. "But it's not been easy. And I'd be lying to you and deceiving myself if I tried to make you believe that I don't have to fight against it. There are times, Felicia, when I get the feeling that I can't hold out for another minute."

"I don't know anything about the hold drugs can get on a person," Felicia said, "so I can only guess what agony you're going through. But I do know God can give you the courage and the strength you need to keep yourself free of drugs."

Shirley relaxed slightly. "I know that. How well I know it. Honestly, Felicia, I wouldn't have been able to last a week if it weren't for the help Jesus Christ gives me."

Felicia glanced down at the speedometer, then said, "Say, Shirley, you mentioned tonight about being saved and how glad you are to know the Lord, but

I don't think I've ever heard how you *did* get saved. What's the story?"

"At the church tonight, I told the kids about getting to the place where I didn't have anywhere else to turn except to God," she began thoughtfully. "Well, I didn't know much about God before that. We went to Sunday school when I was little, but as soon as I got old enough, I stayed home like my parents did. I started fooling around with weed and speed and finally heroin. I felt trapped in a living nightmare. It wasn't long until I got so desperate to be free of the stuff that I–I tried to kill myself."

Felicia nodded. Shirley hadn't actually told the kids that she attempted to take her life, but she had hinted at it.

"One night I decided that I just couldn't take it any longer. I got Mom's bottle of sleeping pills and took all of them. My parents came home earlier than I expected, and they found me unconscious in the living room. They rushed me to the hospital, and the staff there had quite a fight to keep me breathing. Was I mad when I came to and realized I was still alive!"

Shirley paused to chuckle at this memory, and Felicia laughed with her.

"Since I had attempted suicide, I was automatically placed in the psychiatric ward. Dad didn't like that one bit – he was afraid it would hurt his professional image – but there wasn't much he could do about it, in spite of his ranting and raving and

Mom's constant weeping." Shirley paused to laugh at the mental picture of her father storming around the hospital. After a minute, she continued her story.

"It turns out that the psychiatric ward was the best thing that could have happened to me, even though Dad still doesn't see it that way. There was a Christian nurse there – Miss Howes – who really cared about each of the patients. I used to laugh at her when she would tell me that she was praying for me. But I watched her constantly. It was easy to see that there was something different about her – she had such peace and assurance. Finally, I started listening to what she had to say. She showed me that Christ was the answer to all my problems. She helped me to see that He alone could free me from the grip of drugs. Her life had already shown me that she had found the answer that I needed, so, at last, I turned my life over to Him."

"That's really great, Shirley!" Felicia exclaimed.

"Of course, my problems weren't over yet. Attempted suicide is sometimes a crime, so I faced the very real possibility of being sent to juvenile detention, especially since I had been taking drugs."

"Don't keep me in suspense! What happened?"

"Well, the Lord took care of that too. I had a Christian judge, and when he found out that I had gotten saved in the hospital and that I had given my life to the Lord, he gave me a suspended sentence."

"It sure is wonderful to see how the Lord takes

care of things, isn't it? But how did you happen to enroll at Wellington?"

"Miss Howes – that's the Christian nurse who helped me find the Lord – told me it was the place to go. Several of her friends had been students here a few years ago. She said it was a Christian school where I'd have Bible training and get the help from the other girls that I would need."

Felicia winced. She hadn't realized the grip that drugs had on Shirley or her dependence on her and Joan and the others at school. She and Joan had unconsciously looked on Shirley's drug addiction as something that was over and done with and no longer had to be considered. It was a shock to realize that it was still very much a problem.

CHAPTER 2

A NEW CHANCE

Shirley Ellis had appeared unannounced at the Wellington School for Girls one morning six weeks before. She poured out to Miss Duncan a pitiful tale of drug addiction, conversion, and the fight she was having against narcotics. Finally, she finished her story and sat back limply, her hands still working nervously and her white-edged lips trembling. She breathed a sigh of relief; then said, "That's my story, Miss Duncan. Can you help me?"

Miss Duncan leaned forward slightly. She had been watching the girl closely as she had given her narration. She was genuinely concerned, but she was also a quietly efficient individual who kept her emotions in check – the prime example of the proper Wellington girl.

"We would like very much to help you, Miss Ellis. Wellington is founded on the principle of Christian love and concern for others. And we all have a great deal of sympathy for the person who has problems. But here we have our other girls to think of, as well. For this reason, we must carefully weigh each application."

Fear shown in Shirley's eyes. "Then you're not going to let me in the school?" she asked hesitantly.

"I didn't say that," Miss Duncan replied. "I only wanted to caution you not to get your hopes too high. We have a certain routine that we must follow regarding applications. We would want to examine references, for example."

Shirley's smile came hesitantly. "If you require references, I won't get in the school, Miss Duncan," she said quietly. "Nobody is going to want to recommend me after the sort of life I've been living."

Miss Duncan's eyes flashed. "I didn't say that we depend solely on recommendations or that we never take a girl whose references aren't above reproach. I simply said that we want to examine references for all prospective students. That applies to you as well as to anyone else."

Hope rested tentatively on Shirley's tense features.

"Do you mean that there is a chance that you will allow me to come here to school even after all I've done?"

Miss Duncan continued to question her pointedly. She wanted to know where she was from, where she had gone to school previously, and what her parents did for a living. She was particularly concerned about Shirley's conversion experience.

She also wanted to know whether the girl's parents were Christians and when she first became concerned about her need to confess her sin and give Christ first place in her life. And she wanted to know the circumstances under which she made her decision for Christ.

As she questioned Shirley, she made notations on the pad at her elbow. At long last, she looked up.

"I think I have enough information at present," she said finally. "I'll give you application forms. You can fill them out and leave them with my secretary if you'd like."

Shirley nodded. "And when do you think you can let me know if I've been accepted or not?"

Miss Duncan frowned her disapproval. She did not like insistence on the part of applicants for admission. The girls should have the proper desire to attend Wellington and have an appreciation for the school and its problems regarding the admission of students. And a Wellington girl must *never* insist on a decision that is hurried or one that bypasses any portion of the regular routine for the consideration of applicants. "I'm sure I can't tell you. We have certain rules and procedures that must be followed by every applicant. When those procedures have been carried out and we have acted on your application, we will notify you."

Shirley blinked back the tears.

"Does that mean I can't come to school until I've been accepted?" Her voice had a tremor in it.

Miss Duncan started to answer her with the proper reply for the circumstances, but there was something in the girl's manner that caused her to pause.

"That is our normal procedure."

"I was afraid of that."

"I said that was our normal procedure, but there are times when we consider making exceptions. Why is it so important to you?"

Shirley cleared her throat nervously. "I know I have no right to talk to you about suspending your regulations for my benefit. I guess I was just thinking of myself."

"Suppose you explain."

"I was thinking that if you could just take me on probation now – subject to the approval of my application, of course – I would be so grateful. I'm sure that if I could be here under the influence of your school and your teachers and students that I–I wouldn't be faced with such a strong temptation to go back to drugs."

Miss Duncan picked up a pencil and twirled it thoughtfully between her fingers. It was obvious that she was impressed by Shirley's hesitant request. Her head bobbed almost imperceptibly.

"Yes, it might, at that, but I must caution you that our girls here at Wellington are very human and no better or worse than the girls you will find in your church back home. It doesn't necessarily follow that being in a place like this will be a good influence on you."

Shirley eyed her questioningly. "I don't believe I understand what you mean."

"It's very simple. We're working with people, not angels. And there are times when we take in girls we should not take in." She stopped talking momentarily, returned the pencil to her desk, and stared at Shirley briefly. "For example, we dismissed a girl not long ago for the use of narcotics. She needed our help desperately, but we were afraid that her continued presence on campus would present a risk to some of our students who might be easily influenced by such a person. So, we finally had to ask her to leave."

The girl was breathing in quick, shallow gasps. "I'd try not to be a temptation to them." She swallowed hard against the lump of ice that was growing in her throat. "In fact, I would try to be the opposite! I'd try to make them understand that using drugs is dumb – the quickest way I know to get into real trouble." She stopped, once more fighting against the tears. "Wherever I've been since I've become a Christian, I've tried to talk with kids about the dangers of narcotics. I've even spoken in some churches."

That seemed to make up Miss Duncan's mind for her. She glanced down at her notes once more and wrote out an admissions slip.

"You understand, of course, that in giving you a probationary acceptance we are in no way jeopardizing our right to reject your application once all the references are in, don't you?"

"Yes, it means you can keep me from getting in the school if you want to or that you can dismiss me at any time you decide I should be dismissed."

"Exactly." She looked down at the signed admissions slip again. She didn't know why she had decided to allow the Ellis girl to stay until her application was processed. She had always prided herself in staying by the exact letter of every rule set up at Wellington. It was the only way to teach discipline and strength of character in the girls. But now, she was going against the very rules she had been so concerned that others live up to. But, she had decided in Shirley Ellis's favor. She didn't know why.

"I'm going to break our regulations and allow you to stay, Miss Ellis, with the understanding that you are on probation. Should it develop that you have not told us the truth, or if your references indicate that it is advisable, we will ask you to leave."

Shirley's hazel eyes gleamed!

"Oh, thank you, Miss Duncan! Thank you!"

CHAPTER 3

OPPORTUNITIES FOR SERVICE

Miss Duncan called Felicia and Joan into her office. "I want to talk to you about Shirley Ellis," she said. "Have you met her yet?"

"No," Felicia answered, "but we've heard about her." She didn't remind Miss Duncan that there were no secrets in the dormitory. Let a new student come in or an old one be dismissed and everyone in the building knew about it before she had time to open her bags.

"Miss Ellis came to me this morning with a very touching story about her fall into drug addiction, her conversion to Christ, and her fight back. I was so impressed by her honesty and her obvious need of help that I bent the rules enough to accept her on probation."

Joan's eyebrows lifted. Most of the time Miss Duncan seemed like a robot, a computer in flesh and blood but with no emotions. Every now and then, however, something happened to make her seem almost human. This was one of those occasions.

"Is there something we can do to help her?" Felicia asked.

Miss Duncan nodded. "She's a brave little thing with the courage and spunk we like to see in a Wellington girl. In other words, she's got the qualities that can be refined and developed into a resourceful, poised young woman who will be a credit to our school and an effective servant of Christ. But she needs help, and I feel that you two are best able to give it to her."

She went on to tell them about Shirley's experimentation with drugs and her eventual addiction to heroin.

"I have warned her not to talk about this with any of the other students, and I'm going to ask you to do the same," Miss Duncan said, "at least for a time – until we see whether she actually has the qualities I thought I saw in her. We don't want the girls going to her and questioning her about the use of narcotics."

They both agreed.

"What do you want us to do?" Felicia asked her again.

"I think you can be a big encouragement to her by befriending her and helping her to get active in the youth group at the church you attend. She's got to have Christian friends now if she's going to be able to fight against her addiction successfully."

Felicia and Joan talked about going directly to Shirley's room from Miss Duncan's private office but decided against it. Half the girls in the dorm already knew that they had been called into Miss Duncan's office. If they went straight to Shirley's room, they would surmise that Miss Duncan had asked them to. And that would only increase the talk about Shirley. There was always enough talk about every new midterm student without the added fuel of Miss Duncan's concern.

They waited until dinnertime that night before seeking out Shirley. She was with her new roommate, Karen Jennings, who had entered school two weeks before at the beginning of second semester.

"Hi, Karen," Felicia said. "Are these places taken?"

"Not unless you two take them," she replied, cheeks dimpling.

She introduced them to Shirley Ellis.

"We're so glad to know you." Their smiles were genuine.

Miss Duncan had said that the marks of drug addiction were still evident in the new student. The girls saw that she had once been pretty and probably would be again if she could withstand the devastating pull of heroin. Right now, she was far too thin, for one thing. Her skin was sallow, and her eyes were vacant. And there were times when Shirley fell silent. But for all of that, there was strength in her firm, youthful mouth; strength and quiet dignity. It was as Miss Duncan said, Shirley Ellis possessed the qualities of a proper Wellington girl.

Felicia and Joan sat at the table with the other two, carrying on an animated but careful conversation, keeping the talk casual. They asked Shirley about the subjects she would be taking, her special interests and hobbies, and where she lived. Twice, a tenseness seemed to tighten the muscles at the corners of her eyes.

"You wouldn't think she is any different from any of the other students, would you?" Felicia asked her roommate when she and Joan were alone together.

"If we didn't know Miss Duncan was telling us the truth, we'd probably think all of that talk about Shirley was rumor."

It was easy to get to know Shirley, and, in the next few weeks, they grew so close to her that they counted her as one of their best friends. She would pop into their room at all hours to borrow a dictionary or some paper or just to have a cup of tea or a cold drink. On those occasions, she was as casual and relaxed as they were themselves.

At other times, however, a certain moodiness gripped her, and she would sit by the window, staring emptily out at the cold late-winter street. When that happened, she didn't talk to anyone, not even Felicia and Joan.

No one at school found out about Shirley's past until the little prayer group she belonged to had a testimony meeting. She was just coming out of one of those periods of melancholy when the opportunity came for her to speak.

"I suppose you're all wondering why I came to Wellington two weeks past midterm," she said, suddenly feeling the need to tell everyone in the group what God had done for her in sending Christ to save her. "But I am probably not what you think I am."

Felicia tried frantically to catch her eye and warn her to silence, but it was too late. Before Shirley even saw her gesturing, she had told them that she was a drug addict. Several in the group gasped, and the face of one girl went ashen.

The silence in the little room was taut with emotion. And when she continued, they all leaned forward, straining to catch every word. Although Shirley did not spare herself in relating the past, she did not glorify the sort of life she used to lead. In fact, she made it seem even more sordid and unlovely as she went along. And when she spoke of Christ's love for her in spite of her sin, there was a glow in her cheeks.

As soon as Miss Duncan was in her office the following morning, Shirley went in and told her what had happened. The dean of women's smile was reassuring.

"I'm glad you came to me about this, Shirley," she said. "I wondered if you wouldn't."

Shirley stared at her. "You mean you *knew*?"

"I know most things that happen here at the school," Miss Duncan told her.

"I'm really sorry that I violated your trust in me," Shirley went on. "I didn't mean to tell the girls about my experiences with drugs, but they popped out while I was giving my testimony. My heart was so full, I got carried away and said things I didn't plan to say – things I had promised you I wouldn't tell anyone here at school." Concern leaped to her eyes, as though she half expected to be dismissed for it.

But Miss Duncan's smile was pleasant and understanding. Even before she spoke, Shirley knew that she was going to experience no trouble from that direction.

"That's quite all right," the dean of women told her. "I know how such things can happen at testimony meetings where there is a small group, and the Lord is so very close and personal to each one there. I'm sure no harm will come from this." She reached out and touched Shirley's hand lightly with her own. "On the contrary, I think this could work for good among our girls."

Shirley said no more to anyone about her past, but word spread among the girls. It wasn't long until she was called by the youth director of a neighboring church and asked to come over and speak at a Thursday night meeting. Miss Duncan was glad for the opportunity Shirley had to give her testimony but wasn't sure she could suspend the rules to permit it.

"You would have to come back to the dorm after hours alone, and we have never permitted any of our girls to do that."

Disappointment clouded Shirley's attractive young face. "I can't ask you to allow me to break your rules, but I would like to talk to the kids if I could. I might be able to help some of them."

Miss Duncan nodded crisply. "Of course, if Felicia and Joan would consent to go with you, we could make an exception in your case."

Shirley's hazel eyes brightened. "Then I can go?"

"I'll talk with Felicia and Joan about it this afternoon."

The girls were glad to accompany their new friend on her first speaking engagement and came back to the school thrilled with the way she had touched her listeners.

"She did a terrific job, Miss Duncan," they told the dean of women.

"I'm glad to hear your reaction. I completely agreed with it."

"You?" Joan's eyes rounded. "Were *you* at the youth meeting last night?"

"A Wellington girl was speaking, Joan. It was my responsibility to find out if she is doing a creditable job of speaking."

Before the end of the week, Shirley was asked to

go to a church about twenty-five miles west of the school. From then on, she was asked to speak so often that she wasn't able to accept all the opportunities.

Either Felicia or Joan, and sometimes both, accompanied her on such trips. And afterward, they went to see Miss Duncan to tell her about it. Not that she was spying on the new student or even suspicious of her.

"I'm pulling for Shirley all the way," she said, a smile creeping over her austere features. "But I'm interested in what she says in her talks and the way her audiences respond." As she spoke, she formed a church steeple with her fingers. "As I look on it, these speaking engagements of Shirley's are a form of ministry for Wellington. They are part of our contribution to the community around us."

The meeting one particular Sunday night was most effective. Shirley's speech was little different than before, but the question-and-answer time was spirited and forceful. It seemed to Felicia that the kids were much more responsive than at any other place where she had heard Shirley speak. She told Joan all about it that night when she got back to their room and decided to go in the following morning and tell Miss Duncan. "I think she's more interested in Shirley than in any other new student who's come in a long time," Felicia said.

CHAPTER 4

SURPRISING VISITORS

They looked for Miss Duncan in the dining hall that morning at breakfast but didn't see her; so they stopped in at her office when they finished eating. Her secretary hadn't come in yet, but the dean of women heard them in the outer office and invited them to come in.

"I'm so glad you came in to see me this morning. I was about to send for you, Felicia," Miss Duncan said, excitement glittering in her eyes.

Felicia and Joan both squirmed uncomfortably. It was usually not a good sign when the dean of women sent for anyone.

"Is there something wrong?"

"Not at all." Her smile was reassuring. "I just wanted to get your impression of the meeting last night. You see, I already had one phone call about it a few minutes ago."

She told Felicia and Joan that the pastor of the church where Shirley had spoken was so thrilled about her presentation of the drug problem that he and his wife had difficulty sleeping afterward.

"He tells me they have had some unpleasant experiences with drugs in their community, even among some of the church young people, and he's been most anxious that they get the correct story on the subject from someone they respect and will listen to."

"They listened, all right," Felicia told her. "And they asked some serious questions that showed how concerned they actually were. Shirley really got through to them."

On other occasions, that report would have been sufficient for Miss Duncan, and she would have started to ruffle papers or play with a pen to indicate that the interview was over. On this occasion, however, she seemed to have plenty of time and wanted to keep on talking. She asked about the size of the group and the average age and wanted to know the approximate ages of those who asked the most questions.

"This is strictly off the record," Miss Duncan said, "but we're considering a radical departure from policy. We are considering a special assembly program with Shirley as the speaker. There are those of us on the faculty who feel that our Wellington girls could be made aware of the insidious nature of drugs and the terrible results that can come from them."

Before either Joan or Felicia had an opportunity

to reply, there was a slight commotion at the secretary's desk in the outer office. Conversation choked off suddenly, snatched from their lips by the crisp masculine voices outside Miss Duncan's door.

"I don't care if Miss Duncan *is* busy, we've come to talk with her, and we don't have time to wait. Would you please tell her that there is someone out here to see her?"

At the first sound of the man's voice, Miss Duncan stirred slightly, eyelids narrowing. Felicia and Joan had difficulty in controlling the smiles that wanted to lift the corners of their mouths. If there was anything Miss Duncan didn't like, it was someone who tried to barge in without an appointment.

It was probably someone selling something, Felicia reasoned. And, if it was, she could tell them right now that they wouldn't have any success with Miss Duncan. She didn't go for that sort of thing!

Annoyance marked Miss Duncan's face. "Let's see, what was it that we were talking about?"

Joan, however, could not resist mentioning the disturbance to her. "It sounds as though you have someone who wishes to see you, Miss Duncan," she reminded her impishly.

The dean of women scowled. "Whoever it is, he can wait until we've finished our discussion. I have no appointment with the gentlemen out there or with anyone else at this hour."

But the callers in the outer office were not to be

pushed aside so easily. "Listen, miss," the same masculine voice continued, "please tell Miss Duncan that Sidney Larramore and Phillip Miles need to see her immediately."

"I have orders not to disturb Miss Duncan unless the visitor has a confirmed appointment."

"Maybe you would like to take a look at our credentials."

All was silent except for a gasp of surprise from the dean of women's secretary. Then Miss Hanson said quickly, "I'll be glad to call Miss Duncan." She pressed a button on the intercom and said, "Miss Duncan, there are some gentlemen here to see you, and they insist on seeing you immediately."

"I'm busy all morning, Miss Hanson. Tell them they will have to come back after lunch."

"But, Miss Duncan, they're from the United States Drug Enforcement Administration!"

CHAPTER 5

DRUGS AT WELLINGTON?

Miss Duncan pulled in a thin breath of air, and her fingers relaxed. "Have them wait," she said uneasily. "I'll see them in a moment or two."

"That's better. Thank you." Larramore was talking to Miss Hanson, but his voice carried into Miss Duncan's private office on the intercom.

The dean of women sat for a moment, staring beyond the girls at the wall with its picture of the Wellington campus hanging in the middle. It was one of the few times Felicia and Joan had ever seen her reveal her emotions.

"I'm sorry, girls," she managed at last, "but I must conclude this interview. I will have to see these gentlemen immediately."

Felicia and Joan got reluctantly to their feet.

"Is there something we can do to help?" the Cartright girl asked.

Miss Duncan shook her head. "I'm sure that this isn't anything you would be able to help us with. It's probably just routine."

Felicia took a step toward the door. Joan was right behind her but turned back.

"Do you suppose this has anything to do with Shirley Ellis?" she whispered.

Miss Duncan regarded her obliquely. "I haven't the faintest idea."

She walked as far as the door with the girls and opened it. "Thank you for stopping by."

As Felicia left the office of the dean of women, her gaze swept the lean, dark figures of Larramore and Miles. Both men were taller than the average, with piercing eyes.

"Miss Duncan," they heard her secretary say as they passed by and into the corridor, "these gentlemen are here to see you."

"I know." She turned to the visitors, her manner grimly proper. "Won't you come in?"

A moment later, the door closed behind them.

Felicia and Joan paused tensely, pushing their heads even closer together.

"Did you get a look at those two?" Felicia wanted to know.

Joan shuddered. "I'd hate to have them after me, I can tell you that much. They look as though they'd stay after a person until they got what they wanted."

Felicia nodded almost imperceptibly. "They sure do. But what do you suppose this is all about?"

The frown lines around Joan's mouth deepened.

"The only thing I can think of is that they've got some sort of charge against Shirley. You don't suppose they're going to arrest her, do you?"

Felicia gasped sharply. That would be possible, she had to admit. There were a lot of things they didn't know about Shirley. Actually, there was very little that they knew about her beyond the fact that she came to the school with a story of narcotics addiction and a new faith in Jesus Christ. Perhaps she had been involved in selling drugs. Or maybe she induced others to use them in order to pay for her own addiction.

Felicia knew that the whole business of narcotics was one rotten mess, and a person who got involved in it in one way was apt to get sucked into other, more ugly facets.

"You know what I would like to do," Joan said after a time. "I'd like to sneak back into Miss Hanson's office and see if we could hear what those two government agents are saying to Miss Duncan."

Felicia eyed her obliquely. "I'd like to do it, too, but you know about how long we'd last at it and what she would say when we were discovered. We'd really be in trouble."

"You can say that again. A proper Wellington girl does not eavesdrop on any conversation."

"Right. You get a passing grade in manners and conduct."

Joan shook her head. "You know, I get *so* tired of being a proper Wellington girl all the time."

In spite of her concern about the two men in Miss Duncan's office, Felicia laughed. Joan was the best friend she had ever had, but even she wouldn't claim that Joan had ever been the proper Wellington girl and, especially, at all times.

"I'd still like to know what's going on in that office right now."

"So would I, but I guess that isn't going to do us any good."

At that moment, Shirley came hurrying up to them, eyes bright with the joy of living. "Hello, you two. I've been looking all over for you. Where've you been?"

Felicia eyed her uneasily. "We had to see Miss Duncan about something."

"*You* had to see Miss Duncan?" Shirley exclaimed. "Now, if it were just Joan, I could understand that."

The other girl flushed. "What makes you think that I would be so apt to be in trouble?"

"Isn't that the way it is?"

"I wouldn't know about that."

Shirley laughed. "Everybody at school knows about your grade problems." She giggled merrily. "When I first came, some of the girls told me that Miss Duncan was thinking of installing an intercom in your room so she could call you down to her office easier. She said that her secretary spends so much time running after you to come to the office that she can't get her work done."

Joan glanced at Felicia. "You've been talking," she said without anger.

"On my honor."

Joan pulled in a deep breath. "Well, for your information, that wasn't the reason behind our visit at all. Miss Duncan just wanted to talk to us."

Shirley's pretty young face grew serious. "I suppose the subject of your conversation with Miss Duncan is classified." The question hung in Shirley's voice, gently asking for an answer.

Felicia winced at the look in the girl's eyes. Did she know the purpose for their trip to Miss Duncan's office? If she did, what about Larramore and Miles? Did she know about them too? Was her banter genuine, or was she fishing for information?

* * *

Miss Duncan invited the two men from the DEA into her office and closed the door behind them. She went back to her desk without speaking and sat down.

"Now," she said, with all the consideration a proper Wellington girl should show her guests, "what can I do for you?" Her manner did not betray her concern.

Larramore whipped a thin leather folder from an inside jacket pocket, opened it, and held it out to her.

"My name is Sidney Larramore," he said, "from the DEA, and my companion is Phillip Miles."

Miss Duncan examined their credentials carefully.

"You said you wanted to see me," she repeated. "I can't imagine how I could possibly be of assistance to the DEA. We operate a girls' school for the education and training of Christian young ladies. I can see nothing that we would have in common with your department."

Larramore allowed himself a brief smile, as though each one had to be carefully rationed to make them last.

"I can quite understand your bewilderment." He leaned forward, lowering his voice so he could not be heard beyond the room. "Frankly, we were almost as stunned as you must be when we learned through an informer that your school is being used as a drop for narcotics."

In spite of her studied composure, Miss Duncan started. "You can't be serious."

Larramore said quickly, "We are quite sure of it."

Miles broke in. "And don't forget. The smuggling of heroin and pushing it is serious business."

Miss Duncan was not to be intimidated. "I quite agree with you," she retorted evenly. "But it is also serious business to make an accusation against an individual or an institution without definite proof of involvement."

"That's the reason we have come to you," Larramore told her. "We have proof that your school is being used as a narcotics drop."

"And exactly how is this being accomplished?"

He delayed answering for the space of half a minute, eyeing the dean of women dubiously. "I can trust you to be discreet with this information?"

"Young man," Miss Duncan huffed, "I was practicing discretion when you were playing with blocks. Discreet, indeed!"

In spite of the serious tone of the interview, both Larramore and Miles laughed.

"According to our information," the former told her, keeping his voice just above a whisper, "the heroin has been coming in to your school. We haven't yet discovered how."

Miss Duncan was visibly shaken. "Do you mean to tell me that someone in our student body is receiving heroin and selling it?"

"We're talking about something larger than an individual pusher. If our suspicion is correct, one of your students is receiving narcotics on a large scale. The school is a cover for a wholesale drop operation."

"That can't be," Miss Duncan told him. "I have confidence in our girls."

"And we hope that our investigation will prove

that you are correct. You wouldn't want this sort of thing to go on unchecked, would you?"

"Of course not. We're as eager as you are to ferret out any kind of wrongdoing that may be going on here on campus. And we'll be glad to cooperate with you in any way that we can."

"Thank you," Miles answered, the hard lines of his face cracking slightly.

"Yes," Larramore added, "we are grateful for your cooperation." He glanced at his watch as though suddenly remembering that he was running late. "I would like to have a list of the students who attended here at the opening of the current school year and any dropouts or additions since."

Miss Duncan rang for her secretary and asked her to get the information Larramore requested. She sat stiffly in her chair, watching them closely as they studied the list.

"I doubt that you will find anything there that will be of help to you."

"Possibly. Possibly not."

Several minutes passed before he spoke again. "Oh, here's an interesting name: Carol Groves."

Miss Duncan flinched. "She no longer goes to school here."

"I'm aware of that. She was dismissed for the use of narcotics, wasn't she?"

"That's right. She was accepted on probation and was here for approximately two months. When she came in, we knew that she had been dabbling with drugs, but she assured us that this part of her life was behind her, so we gave her an opportunity to prove herself."

Before she even finished what she was saying, Larramore was nodding as though he already had the information she was giving him. As soon as she realized that, she stopped. "Apparently you know all about Miss Groves."

"We know more about Carol Groves than you do. You see, we have a dossier on her. There was a time, before she was dismissed from school, when we were sure that *she* was our guilty party."

"In fact," Miles said, "we still strongly suspect that she was placed here on your campus for that very purpose, but she couldn't refrain from using drugs herself, and you dismissed her before we were able to get the evidence we needed to close down the operation."

Miss Duncan inhaled deeply. She knew the narcotics agents were only doing their jobs, and she was as anxious as they were to uncover *any* sort of drug smuggling that might involve the school. Yet, she found it vaguely disturbing to know that they had so much information about a former Wellington student. She wondered what they knew about the others.

"Have you heard that Miss Groves died last week from an overdose of heroin?" Larramore asked, his voice flat and expressionless.

Miss Duncan gasped.

"She died a week ago yesterday in County Hospital. Apparently, she got a dose of heroin that was too pure. She was in terrible shape when they brought her in. Didn't live an hour."

"How horrible!"

"It is that," Larramore exclaimed. "It's a horrible, rotten business."

Miss Duncan was not even listening. She was thinking of Carol Groves, who had seemed to be so determined to give up narcotics when she came into the school seeking admittance. And they had failed her! Somehow – in some way – they hadn't been able to get through to Carol. What had gone wrong?

She remembered how thoroughly they had discussed the girl and how reluctant they had been to dismiss her. The decision had been based on the need to protect the other girls who might be susceptible to experimenting with narcotics. But did that relieve them of their responsibility to one who was already addicted? Should they have tried harder to reach her?

A question from Larramore brought her attention back to him. "We know about a number of these students," he said, "but we would like a bit more information on some of them."

"I'll supply it if I can."

The two men talked with Miss Duncan for another twenty minutes, going over the names that Larramore wanted to learn more about. At last, he seemed to be satisfied, and putting the list into the briefcase he was carrying, he acted as though he was about to leave.

"We do want to thank you for your help."

"That's quite all right." She had regained her composure and was the example of calm, unruffled efficiency that had been a model for Wellington girls for many, many years. "Is there anything else we can help you with?"

Larramore frowned.

"As a matter of fact, there is something you can help us with. We have a plan for ferreting out the people who are involved in this heroin smuggling ring. However, we are going to need some assistance from the school in order to bring it off."

CHAPTER 6

A SERIOUS MATTER

After the men from the DEA left her office, Miss Duncan remained motionless behind her desk. She had thought that in all her years at the school she could not be shocked by anything, but she had never before faced a situation like this. One former student was dead and who knew how many other lives would be destroyed unless the smuggling of heroin was cut off?

She almost wished that she could close her eyes and make the specter of Larramore and Miles and the threat of adverse publicity for the school disappear. Instantly, she was rebuked. Such a serious matter could not be swept under the rug. It had to be exposed and the guilty ones ferreted out and punished. Even the potential problems the adverse publicity might cause could not be considered.

Miss Hanson came in, curious, trying to learn

more about the purpose of the unexpected visit of the government agents.

"Do those men suspect someone from school of pushing drugs?" she asked in a taut half-whisper.

Miss Duncan turned toward her. "Miss Hanson," she said, "how long have you been my private secretary?"

The other woman caught the tone in the dean's voice. "I'm going on my ninth year," she replied.

"Precisely. And how many times have I told you that the primary virtues of a private secretary are to do as she is told, refrain from curiosity about matters that don't concern her, and to keep anything she hears, sees, or suspects to herself."

Miss Hanson looked down. "I'm sorry," she blurted. "I was just so stunned at having those men introduce themselves as agents of the DEA that I lost control of myself."

"That's quite all right, Miss Hanson," Miss Duncan told her, smiling a bit. "I can well understand. I was startled by the visit myself."

She remained beside Miss Duncan's desk, motionless. "Thank you."

The dean of women picked up a sheaf of papers and directed her attention to them, her standard procedure for dismissing a caller. But her secretary still did not leave.

"Miss Duncan, is everything all right? Are any of our girls in trouble with the law?"

Miss Duncan's gaze remained fixed momentarily.

Then she lifted her head, and her eyes fixed on the person at her elbow.

"Not that I know of, Miss Hanson. At least I hope they aren't."

"So do I."

When her secretary was gone, Miss Duncan frowned thoughtfully. She would have to call Felicia and Joan into her office and warn them to silence. She got her secretary on the intercom and asked her to have them come to her office as soon as they had a free period.

"I'll get word to them immediately."

"Thank you, Miss Hanson."

Felicia and Joan were surprised at being sent for so soon. They stopped briefly at Miss Hanson's desk.

"What's the matter?" Joan asked. "Am I having problems with English again?"

"You'll have to ask Miss Duncan about that. She is the one who had me get in touch with you."

The girls glanced uneasily at each other.

"What do you suppose we've done now?" Joan wanted to know.

The frown lines around Felicia's mouth tightened. "Maybe nothing."

"I would suggest that you go in and find out," Miss Hanson said, smiling.

Miss Duncan was standing beside her desk when they entered her private office, her sturdy face a studied mask of controlled emotion.

"Close the door, please, Felicia." She said no more until that was accomplished and the girls were seated across from her. "I suppose you realize by now that I have called you in because of the two visitors I had earlier this morning."

Joan stared at her. "You mean it isn't because of my grades?"

Miss Duncan ignored her question. "I don't know exactly what you girls heard and what you didn't hear of my conversation with those two men." She paused, waiting for them to supply that information.

"We didn't hear too much," Felicia told her, "except that this Mr. Larramore and Mr. Miles are narcotics agents and they wanted to see you about something quite important."

"That, Felicia, is an understatement. Their visit was *most* important. In fact, one might say that it was of vital importance." She breathed deeply. "You haven't told anyone about it, have you?"

They shook their heads.

"Then I caught you in time. I must ask you not to mention it to anyone else."

"You can depend on us."

"I have decided to share this information with you girls and with Miss Hanson," the dean of women said, "so you will know why it is so important that we keep the story a secret."

She called Miss Hanson into her private office and related the entire story.

"Are we going to do anything about it?" Joan asked when Miss Duncan finished. "I mean, is the school going to do anything about finding out if it's true?"

"We're going to cooperate with the authorities in every way that we can."

"Is there anything we can do to help?" Felicia wanted to know.

The dean of women shook her head. "Not that I know of."

The girls left soon, with Miss Hanson still in Miss Duncan's office.

In comparative silence, the girls left the administration building and crossed the campus to the ivy-covered dormitory where they lived.

"There's got to be something we can do to help," Felicia said at last.

Joan closed and locked the door to their room then pivoted to face her. "Now, wait a minute," she exclaimed. "This isn't the kind of a problem that we've got any business getting mixed up in. I can tell you that right now. The government agents know all about it. Let them take care of it if they want it taken care of."

But Felicia was not so easily dissuaded.

"We're right here at school, Joan. We might be able to find out a lot of things that Mr. Larramore and Mr. Miles wouldn't be able to."

"I doubt that."

"Just the same, we've got to try. We can't let the people who are using Wellington to peddle drugs get away with it. We owe that much to the other young people our age who might get hooked on the terrible stuff. And we owe it to our school to help get this thing straightened out so it won't cause a big scandal for Wellington."

Joan shook her head incredulously. "Here we go again." She gestured her exasperation. "I don't know why I let you talk me into these things. You get me into more trouble than any other ten people I know."

"Be careful now," Felicia countered, laughter dancing in her blue eyes. "A proper Wellington girl doesn't exaggerate."

"A proper Wellington girl doesn't get her room-mate into trouble either. That's for sure."

Felicia scarcely heard her. "It gives me cold chills when I think that somebody who's going to school here is actually working with a gang of heroin smugglers."

Joan went over and plumped herself in a chair. "Knowing about this does make me curious as to who it could be," she murmured thoughtfully.

That was all the agreement Felicia needed. She hitched her chair closer to her friend's and spoke in guarded tones.

"If we get to work, I know we can find out who's guilty."

Joan straightened. "You can't expect much out of me. You're the detective. I just go along to keep you from getting into too much trouble."

"Now where's a good place to start?" Felicia asked.

"Search me."

"How could anyone get the drugs into a school like this?"

Joan was silent momentarily. "It could come in with the meat or milk or bread," she suggested, "or with the janitor supplies."

Felicia sighed. "It could come in a hundred different ways, I suppose."

"You can say that again. There's always someone carrying things into one of the buildings."

Felicia crossed the room slowly, then turned to face her roommate. "Most of the deliveries to the school are handled so carelessly they'd hardly dare to use them. The milk's just brought to the back door and left, and any one of three or four in the kitchen sign for the meat and other food when it comes in."

"That's right. And the other deliveries are usually left outside the door of the department doing the ordering."

"Someone could have a package delivered to her by some store, I suppose," Felicia said. "Or she could act as though it came from a store, and she could be in her room when it arrived, so she'd be sure to get it."

Joan nodded. "That is more logical. It could be mailed in too. There are so many packages coming into the school that no one would think to check them."

"Hmm. That's another possibility." Felicia pulled in a deep breath. "You know, I wish we hadn't had to promise Miss Duncan not to say anything to anyone."

"Why?"

"We could tell Shirley Ellis to keep an eye out for

any suspicious packages that come in. She works in the post office, you know."

"I'd forgotten about that."

"Come to think of it, why do you suppose she was so anxious to get a job in the post office?"

"I didn't know she was," Joan answered. "And I don't know what this has got to do with drugs being brought into the school either."

"Don't you remember how she talked to Miss Duncan about having to have a job if she was going to be able to go to school? And she kept talking about being experienced in handling mail too."

Joan paused. "You aren't saying that Shirley's the one who's having the drugs sent to her, are you?" She lowered her voice self-consciously.

The corners of Felicia's mouth twitched nervously. "All I'm saying is that Shirley does have contact with drugs – or has had. She even used heroin. That means she would have to know some of the people who sell the stuff. They might have talked her into coming here as a student to help handle the heroin."

Joan was slow in replying. "I'd hate to think that after the way she's talked about what God has done for her in helping her to stay off the stuff and after all the talking in churches that she's been doing."

"So would I," Felicia continued. "And maybe there isn't anything to it, but she does have the trust of everyone in the school. It might be easier for her to do it than it would someone else."

CHAPTER 7

A NEW JOB

Joan blinked, but her gaze did not waver from her best friend's serious young face. It didn't seem reasonable to her that Shirley Ellis could have any part in a drug-smuggling operation after testifying so strongly about her new life in Christ and talking so fervently to anyone who would listen to her about the terrible results of using drugs.

"Do you really think Shirley could be mixed up in this rotten business?" she asked.

Felicia hesitated. "I'd hate to think she is. But you've got to admit that this would be an excellent cover for anyone who was trying to avoid being suspected. Don't you agree?"

Joan crossed to a chair near the desk and dropped into it. What Felicia said was true. Talking to everyone the way Shirley had been doing was an excellent way to keep from being suspected herself. And now that she thought about it, it was strange that the new student had applied for work in the mail room.

"The question is," she said aloud, "what are we going to do about it?"

"That's the big question."

"I wish we could go right to Shirley's room and talk to her about it. She might be able to give us a very simple explanation for everything."

"Oh, we can't do that. We gave our word to Miss Duncan that we wouldn't say anything to anyone about the visit of the DEA. Besides, if she was involved, that would give away everything."

"Just what can we do?"

"One of us might get a job in the post office with Shirley," Felicia said. "That way we could keep a close eye on her."

"That might work, at that."

They sat for a long while in their room talking about the post office and how they would go about getting a job there. They talked for so long they almost missed their next class. Joan noted the time and jumped to her feet.

"We'd better get cracking, or we'll be back in Miss Duncan's office again before we know it."

That evening, Felicia and Joan went down the hall to Shirley's room. They had hoped to get a chance to talk to her, to do some gentle prying that might give them a clue as to her involvement in the heroin smuggling ring. Her roommate had several visitors however. The chairs were all in use, and two girls were sitting on Karen's bed.

"Here," Shirley said, laughter tugging upward at the corners of her mouth. "We'll shove those things out of the way so you can sit on my bed."

They could not help laughing, as usual, at the wild assortment of stuffed animals that covered the new student's bed. There were cats and elephants and giraffes and kangaroos in a delightful assortment of colors and shapes.

Joan picked up a yellow koala bear and examined it carefully.

"Isn't he precious?"

"He's one of my favorites," Shirley said. "I got him for Christmas from my boyfriend last year."

Felicia picked up a roguish octopus with tentacles a yard long. It was as soft as cashmere to her touch.

"I suppose your boyfriend gave you this too."

"As a matter of fact, he did. He's got an uncle who's an importer so he can get all sorts of cute little animals for me."

"If you ever get tired of him," Joan said brashly, "let me know. I'd like to pick up a boyfriend like that for a while."

"Wouldn't we all?" Karen laughed.

"When I get tired of him, I'll let you know."

Someone started playing some music. Almost abruptly, the conversation changed to music and was subdued. It was not until later that Karen mentioned the two men who went to Miss Duncan's office that morning.

"I was going down the hall when I almost ran into them."

"Maybe one of them was Shirley's boyfriend."

"Not one of those two," Karen said. "You should have seen their eyes! They looked as though they could stare a hole right through a person."

"Is that what your boyfriend's like?" someone wanted to know.

"I'll never tell." Then Shirley's smile faded. "You and Joan were in Miss Duncan's office this morning before class, Felicia. Did you see those men who frightened Karen so badly?"

Crimson stained Felicia's cheeks. Shirley could be teasing, but there could be something more in her voice as well, an undercurrent that was vaguely disturbing.

"We'll never tell," she murmured, hoping that would be sufficient to stop Shirley's questioning.

"As a matter of fact," Joan blurted, "we're saving them for ourselves – if we can get them away from Miss Duncan, that is."

Karen's eyes rounded. "How do you dare to say things like that?"

"What do you mean?" Joan looked about quickly, half expecting to see someone recording her laughing jest about the dean of women.

"The way Miss Duncan finds out things around

here, I've come to the conclusion that she's positively clairvoyant."

"That's it, Felicia!" Joan cried. "That's the reason Miss Duncan calls me into her office all the time. She's clairvoyant, and we happen to be on the same wavelength or something, so she knows everything I'm thinking."

They all laughed at that, and the conversation was safely steered away from the two men who had come to Miss Duncan's office that morning. Felicia and Joan didn't stay very long after that.

"I've got to get Joan back so she can study her history before class tomorrow."

"There she goes again." Joan shrugged with exaggerated helplessness. "That's the reason I'm never able to take care of myself. Felicia is always fussing about me so much that I don't have any self-confidence."

"We'd better hurry, or it'll be time for lights out and neither one of us will have our history done."

The next morning, Felicia insisted that they go down and tell Miss Duncan about Shirley's interest in the two strangers.

"Do you think we ought to?" Joan asked, her reluctance showing. "After all, it isn't any real evidence. She could have just been curious."

"I know, but with some of these other things and the seriousness of the situation, I think Miss Duncan should know."

Joan thought about that. She didn't like the idea of

tattling on Shirley without more evidence than they had. On the other hand, Miss Duncan was loyal to her girls. She could be trusted to use discretion. Going to her wouldn't be the same as going to Larramore and Miles with the information. She might even be able to use it to help the new student if she was convinced of her innocence. Although Joan didn't quite know how that could be. "I suppose it would be all right," she said aloud.

Felicia's eyes gleamed. "Besides, I've got to have a good reason for seeing Miss Duncan. I've got an idea."

Joan inhaled sharply. "I might have known that you'd get an idea. You couldn't keep out of a mess like this if you wanted to. You've got a devious mind, Felicia. Always scheming."

"How you talk!"

"I mean it. I don't know why I put up with you after all the trouble you've gotten me into. I don't even know why I keep you for a friend."

"I do," Felicia dimpled. "It's because I'm so sweet and kind and considerate."

"And bossy," Joan added, her eyes betraying her playfulness. "You boss me around so much I get to thinking you're Miss Duncan instead of my best friend."

"Quit complaining and come with me. I want to see Miss Duncan before she gets too busy to talk to us."

Felicia needn't have worried about Miss Duncan

not wanting to see them. She asked Miss Hanson to let them into her office immediately.

"And hold all my calls for a few minutes. I don't wish to be disturbed."

"Yes, Miss Duncan." Surprise was etched indelibly on the secretary's severe features, but her voice was inexpressive. She glanced at the girls as though she would like to question them but didn't quite dare. "You may go in now."

The dean of women seemed glad for the opportunity to talk to Felicia and Joan. She made sure that the intercom was turned off and leaned forward.

"Now, what did you want to see me about?" she asked softly.

Felicia told her about going into Shirley's room the night before and the apparent interest the new student showed in Larramore and Miles.

"Did she say anything that would make you think she was unduly interested in them?" Miss Duncan asked.

"Not really. I guess it was more an attitude than anything else. Both Joan and I had the feeling that there was more than curiosity behind her questions."

Miss Duncan nodded thoughtfully. "That could be," she murmured. "That could be. But, of course, we must be very careful not to make an unjust accusation or to consider her guilty."

"That's the reason we came to you, Miss Duncan,"

Felicia told her. "We knew that you would be careful about protecting Shirley."

"But," Joan added, "we thought you ought to know about this."

The dean of women nodded. "I'm very glad that you came to me. It is the sort of thing that should be explored – but cautiously."

She was about to dismiss the girls with the caution to hurry to class when Felicia spoke again.

"There's something else that we've been wondering about. Shirley has a job in the post office here at school. Wouldn't that place her in an excellent position to get any suspicious mail that came in?"

Miss Duncan frowned. "I'm not quite sure about that. There's always a supervisor present when anyone is working. I don't see how she would be able to get her hands on any mail that didn't belong to her."

That stopped Felicia momentarily. She pulled in a deep breath, then exhaled it.

"Perhaps, but what if she has worked out a scheme of getting a package of heroin that came in the mail? Wouldn't it be good to have someone in the post office who was watching her all the time – someone she trusts?"

Miss Duncan smiled faintly. "Do you have anyone in particular in mind? Someone like yourself or Joan, perhaps?"

"How did you know?"

"I've been acquainted with you for quite a while,

Felicia. I should be well aware of your scheming by this time."

Joan faced her friend. "What did I tell you? You're getting a reputation as a conniver."

The laughter left Miss Duncan's eyes. "I think you have an excellent idea, Felicia. It will give us a chance to keep an eye on Shirley without saying anything to anyone else."

She started to make a note on the pad on her desk, then hesitated. "There's one difficulty though. What will the other girls think about your working? You've never had to work during the school year before."

"Joan and I were talking about that last night. We decided that, since my parents' twentieth wedding anniversary really is coming up in a couple of months, I could just say that I wanted to buy them an extra-special gift this year."

The dean of women nodded. "That's a very good idea. Well, I'll take care of this then."

The next day, Felicia was summoned by Miss McGuire and put to work in the school post office. Shirley was delighted with the new development.

"You don't know how happy I am that you'll be working with me, Felicia. This is going to be great."

CHAPTER 8

A STAGED TESTIMONY?

It seemed to Felicia that Shirley was a little more excited about her coming to the post office to work than she would normally be. Felicia wasn't sure, of course, but it seemed as though she was going to great effort to make Felicia think she wanted her. Perhaps just the opposite was true! Miss McGuire had Shirley show Felicia what to do.

"You can start her out the way I started you, Shirley. And after she's learned to sort parcels, you can have her help you with the first-class mail."

Felicia soon learned how to sort the parcels that came for the girls from home and was promoted to working with first-class mail as well. Once she was familiar with the routine, she was put on the outgoing mail, learning how to sort it for pickup by the downtown post office.

Questions still bothered Felicia, but she couldn't

help wondering if the talk about drug smuggling had been an ugly dream.

"Maybe it was somebody's idea of a sick joke," Joan said when she voiced that opinion to her roommate in the quiet of their dormitory room.

"I'd like to believe that," she said, "but I can't help feeling that it's all very real. It isn't the sort of thing people would joke about."

Joan's frown deepened.

"Maybe not, but if it isn't a joke, I think it must be a false alarm. Nothing's happened so far to indicate that it's anything else."

But Felicia was not so sure. "We think nothing's happened because we don't know about it," she said. "But there might be plenty happening right now."

Joan sat down at her desk and flipped her history book open. "I can't understand why anyone would want to use the postal room of a school like Wellington as a drop for narcotics. It just doesn't make sense to me."

"It doesn't make sense to me either," Felicia said. "But the smugglers might figure that this is the last place the authorities would think to look."

They were still talking about it when there was a knock at their door and Shirley burst in. "Oh, I'm so glad you're both here!" Excitement gleamed in her eyes.

"What's the matter? Is there something wrong?"

"I was talking to Karen this evening. Did you know that she's not a Christian?"

The girls both shook their heads. They had to confess that they hadn't gotten to know Karen well enough to find out.

"I had the most exciting talk with her. I gave her my whole testimony from the time I first started fooling around with drugs until I got hooked on heroin. I told her about hearing the gospel for the first time and how I finally gave my heart to Christ. She acted as though she'd never heard anything like it before."

"That's wonderful," Felicia said. "That she would show an interest, I mean."

Shirley sat down, clasping and relaxing her hands. "I suppose it sounds silly to you, but I was so excited after we finished talking that I just had to tell someone about it."

Joan and Felicia both smiled their understanding.

"We know just how it is," the Bailey girl told her. "I'll never forget how excited I was the first time I shared Jesus Christ with anyone. I was so scared when I started that I didn't think I'd be able to finish, but afterward I felt as though someone had just given me a million dollars."

A smile spread across Shirley's face. "I've given my testimony in churches when I've talked about drugs, but this is the first time I've ever talked with one person about her need of Christ. It makes you feel wonderful, doesn't it?"

Before Shirley went back to her room, they prayed together that God would continue to speak to Karen and bring her to the place where she would make her decision for Christ.

"And we'll keep praying for her," Felicia assured their new friend. "We'll be praying for both of you."

"Thank you. Thank you so very much." With that, she was gone.

Joan closed the door behind her thoughtfully. "That was quite a surprise, wasn't it?"

"A wonderful surprise," Felicia repeated.

"A very convenient surprise if you ask me."

Her eyes rounded quizzically. "What do you mean by that, Joan?"

Her roommate went over and sat down. "This might not be fair to Shirley, but let's do a little supposing for a couple of minutes. Just you and me."

Felicia found a chair across from her.

"Now, what if she were actually a part of the drug smuggling ring? She's managed to get herself enrolled as a student at the school they've selected for the drop. She's gotten herself a good cover with her profession of faith in Christ and her talks against drugs and addiction. She's even managed to get herself a job in the school post office, so everything is set for the shipment to come in. Then you're placed in the post office, and she's afraid that they might be suspecting her for what she really is. Doesn't a scene like the one we've just witnessed fit right into that picture?"

Felicia nodded. "Of course, we could go to Karen and see if it's true that Shirley witnessed to her just now."

"Oh, I'm sure she did," Joan continued quickly. "She wouldn't be careless enough to say she had when she hadn't, and we could find out if she was lying."

"What you're saying, then, is that Shirley staged this for our benefit. She did it because she wanted to be able to tell us about it."

"Exactly."

Felicia had to admit that the circumstantial evidence that was building against Shirley was formidable, indeed. Much more so than when she used it to get Miss Duncan to put her to work in the post office.

"But I'd hate to believe that Shirley would be so brazen and two-faced. I really would. I've got more confidence than that in her."

"So do I. I was just supposing." She drew in a long breath. "But, when you think about it that way, it sure doesn't sound good for Shirley."

Felicia found it difficult to sleep that night. Every time she closed her eyes, she could see her new friend's serious young face turned up to hers and could hear her excited voice as she told about her roommate's interest in Jesus Christ. And then Felicia would writhe under the dark stare of Larramore and Miles. Those two characters had a way of ruining everything. In that moment, it was almost as though they were at fault because of the threat they posed to the school's well-ordered little world.

The next morning when she got up, Felicia had the same feeling as before – that there was no reality to the drug-smuggling ring or Shirley's possible involvement. It was all a grim, senseless joke or a dream that was over, now that she was awake. Unfortunately, it was all too true.

Shirley was more open and friendly than before, if that were possible. She often came into their room to talk with them about the progress she was making with Karen.

"Karen acted as though she didn't want to talk to me about Jesus Christ at first," she told them, "but last night I had another opportunity to have a long, serious talk with her. She's doing some serious thinking now about the things I've told her."

"How wonderful."

Her eyes gleamed as she asked them to keep on praying for her roommate. They promised her they would.

Felicia worked with Shirley every day in the school post office, and she and Joan spent as much free time as possible with the girl. As often as they could, they visited her in her room, and occasionally they took her out with them for a dish of ice cream. She was still speaking publicly as much as usual, and they accompanied her on those trips.

Shirley was interesting to be with, and, in spite of the tension that swirled around her, she seemed to be as happy and carefree as any other girl on the campus. She was always able to laugh about something, which made her a lot of fun. For that reason, both Felicia and Joan were astonished when Karen knocked lightly on the door and half whispered, "Can you come with me and see if you can do something for Shirley?"

Felicia's eyes rounded. "Shirley!" she gasped. "What's the matter with her?"

"I don't know. But, please come!" Desperation twisted her pretty, young face.

CHAPTER 9

SHIRLEY'S STORY

Felicia and Joan hurried down the corridor with Karen.

"I had to go to the library this evening," she explained on the way. "And she was all right when I left. But when I got back, she was lying on the bed sobbing, and I can't get her to stop. She's been crying for an hour!"

Felicia paused just inside the door, looking down at the girl sprawling on the bed. Shirley's shoulders were shaking so convulsively, and she was crying so hard that she did not even know anyone else had come into the room.

"Shirley," Joan said, her voice gentle and soothing. "Shirley."

No answer.

Felicia moved to the bed and sat down beside her, placing a comforting hand on her shoulder.

"Shirley, is there anything we can do to help?"

The new student seemed to be aware of her presence. Her shoulders stopped shaking briefly, and she mumbled something unintelligible.

"What is it, Shirley? What's wrong?"

She tried to speak but, after a word or two, began to sob once more.

"I've been trying to find out what's troubling her," Karen said helplessly, "but I couldn't get anywhere with her. She's been crying like that for an hour."

After her first attempt to get Shirley to tell them what was wrong, Felicia sat beside her quietly. For the space of several minutes, no one spoke. At last, however, the distraught girl was able to stop crying enough to sit up and wipe at the tears that still dribbled out of her eyes and moistened her cheeks.

"Here," Felicia said, "here's a tissue."

Shirley pushed herself half around to face her blonde friend. "I–I'm sorry to be making such a fool of myself," she stammered.

"You didn't make a fool of yourself. We only wish that there was something we could do to help."

Her voice fell away into silence, and the girls looked at Shirley and each other helplessly. They felt so inadequate – so unable to do anything to ease the hurt she must be experiencing.

Joan coughed nervously, and Karen went over to the window to adjust the shade; not because there was anything wrong with it, she just had to have something to do. Felicia's eyes caught Shirley's and held them captive.

"We can't do anything for you unless we know what's bothering you so terribly," she said, a firmness creeping into her voice.

"I–I don't think there's anything that you – or anyone else – can do to help." She started to sniffle again. "This is something that I'm going to have to work out for myself."

Felicia glanced quickly, questioningly, at Joan. Could that mean what she thought it might mean?

"We would like to try it," she said gently.

That seemed to help Shirley reach a decision. She shoved her shoulders back and began bravely, "I–I've been debating doing something that I've finally decided I have to do."

She started to sniffle again, her throat constricting until she found it difficult to speak. "I'll try, but I don't know whether I can manage it or not."

The girls waited patiently for her to continue.

"I think I told you that I've been dating a boy from my hometown for the last year or so. I guess Pete and I always thought that we would be married someday. Then I became a Christian, and he didn't like that much. He was afraid that it was going to take me away from him."

"If you really love him," Karen broke in, "I don't see why a little thing like religion would interfere."

Shirley's gaze found her momentarily, but she did not reply to her.

"I used to tell Pete that nothing in all the world could break us up, but the last few weeks I–" She choked again until she could not go on. It was some-time later before she could talk once more. Then she told them that she had finally reached the place where she had realized that she couldn't go on the way she had been. She had to give up Pete Cameron.

"So," she went on, forcing out the words, "I wrote him a letter telling him that I couldn't see him again. I mailed it just before dinner this evening." Her smile winked bravely. "After I got back here to the room, I guess I got to feeling sorry for myself. I got to wondering whether I did the right thing or not. That's why I said that this was something I'd have to work out for myself."

"I can understand how you feel," Felicia told her. "But I'm sure you'll realize later that you've done what you had to do. You couldn't keep dating a per-son who isn't a Christian."

Karen eyed her roommate and Felicia quizzically.

"I've never heard anything so stupid," she said. "If you love him, why not be with him? I can't blame him for being uptight about it if religion means more to you than he does."

Hurt showed in Shirley's eyes. "When you say it that way, you make me feel so–so unfair to him."

"And I think you have been unfair to him," Karen

continued, glancing defiantly at Joan and Felicia. "I know *they* won't agree with me. They're hung up on religion too. But I can't help it. I've got to tell you exactly how I feel. I wouldn't give up a boyfriend because of religion, that's for sure."

"It wouldn't make any difference if you dated a boy who isn't a Christian or not," Felicia said quietly.

Karen's eyes narrowed. "What do you mean by that?"

"The Bible says that we aren't to be unequally yoked with unbelievers," she went on. "So, since you aren't a Christian yourself, it doesn't make any difference who you date. That verse is only for a child of God."

Karen jerked to face Felicia.

"I don't know whether I like that or not," she retorted testily. "I'm just as good as Shirley or either of you two."

"I'm sure you are," Felicia agreed with her.

That seemed to surprise Karen. She jerked upright, eyes widening.

"The only difference is that we've confessed our sin and asked God to save us through Jesus Christ. We've been given new lives."

Karen settled back in her chair, thoughtfully.

It was Joan who finally suggested that they have a cup of coffee.

"I'm sorry," Karen said, stirring, "but we don't have any."

"I'll go down to our room and get some. I might even be able to scare up a few cookies."

While the water was heating, Felicia and Joan encouraged Shirley to talk about Peter Cameron and the decision she had made. While she told how she had first met Pete and started going out with him, Karen slumped in her chair, studying the carpet intently.

"I've never told anyone this," Shirley concluded. "I've been too ashamed to, but Pete was the one who first got me using weed. I didn't want to, but he kept after me until I tried marijuana at one of his parties one night."

Karen flinched. "You mean your boyfriend wanted you to use weed? I can hardly believe it."

"It's true, just the same. He was one of those people who could use weed and stop with that, but I couldn't. I had to keep getting stronger and stronger drugs until, finally, I was addicted to heroin."

Felicia glanced obliquely at Shirley's roommate.

"I'm sure that this is the sort of thing God wants us, as Christians, to guard against."

"Now wait a minute," Karen broke in. "Not every non-Christian boy would get his date started on weed. They aren't all that low."

"Weed is only one thing," Felicia said, "an example of what I was talking about. Some boys who aren't Christians don't drink or smoke, but they might influence a Christian girl away from Christ or even keep her from going to church. There are good reasons why the Bible tells us not to go with unsaved guys."

Joan read a chapter of the Word of God, and the three of them prayed together while Karen looked on stonily. Then, shortly before lights out, Felicia and Joan went back to their room.

"I'm so glad you girls came to see me," she said, managing to smile a little. "I feel much better about everything now."

"We're glad for that."

When they were back in their room alone, Felicia turned to Joan. "That was something, wasn't it?"

"When Shirley said she had a problem, I had no idea that it was that kind of a problem. I thought it was something else."

Felicia's lips tightened painfully. "So did I. But I finally have come to the conclusion that she must be sincere." Her voice firmed as she spoke. "I'm convinced now that she isn't mixed up in that smuggling deal that's got everybody so shaken up."

A faraway look gleamed in Joan's eyes. "I hope you're right," she murmured, doubt edging her voice. "I really hope you're right. But I can't help thinking about Carol Groves and how she deceived everybody around here."

"But she didn't profess to be a Christian, and Shirley does."

"I know," Joan answered, "but that could be part of the act. Don't forget that."

Felicia was still unconvinced that Shirley would have any part in smuggling anything, let alone heroin, but it didn't do any good to argue with Joan about it. She had her mind made up, and she wouldn't think otherwise until Felicia, or someone, had proved that she was wrong.

The thin line of her mouth hardened. She didn't care what Joan said. She was sure Shirley wasn't mixed up with the smugglers, and she wasn't going to stop until she had proved her new friend's innocence.

The following day, the girls thought Shirley would be feeling much better. A good night's rest, they reasoned, would give her an entirely new outlook on the problem she faced. However, when they stopped to get her to go to breakfast with them, her roommate said she was still in bed with a blinding headache.

"Oh, that's too bad," Felicia said.

"You probably think you helped her," Karen said accusingly, "but I think you did the opposite. You just about broke her heart telling her that she ought to give up her boyfriend."

Felicia started to reply but read the hostility in Karen's eyes and changed her mind.

"She's more upset about having to give up her boyfriend than she'll ever let on to you."

"Will she be going to classes today?" Felicia asked.

"I'm not at all sure," Karen answered primly. "I know that I wouldn't if I were as upset as she is."

However, when Felicia went to the school post

office to work that morning, she was surprised to see Shirley there.

"I didn't think you would be working today," Felicia said to her.

"Because of my headache?" she asked. "I got to feeling better, so I decided to come to my second period class and then over here."

"I'm so glad, Shirley."

"There's no use in letting it get me down. I've got to keep going, regardless of how I feel about Pete."

"Do you still feel the way you did last night?"

"Oh, yes." Shirley seemed surprised that she would ask. "I certainly do, in spite of what Karen said to me about it."

Felicia went back to work, relieved at the new Christian's attitude. Few girls would be able to accept such a blow as bravely as she was.

The girls had sorted the first-class mail and were starting on the parcels when Felicia found a package with the name and part of the address torn off.

"What's this?" she asked aloud, holding up the parcel.

Shirley and Miss McGuire glanced up quickly. "Who does it go to?" Shirley wanted to know.

"That's what I'm wondering. It doesn't say who it's from or who it goes to."

CHAPTER 10

THE PINK POODLE!

Felicia and Shirley examined the package more carefully. It looked very much like any other package that came in to the school. It was of average size, the sort of package that could contain a cake or cookies or some new clothes. It was wrapped in brown paper. The name of the one who was to receive it was half obliterated. Only part of the address remained.

"I can't make out who's supposed to get it," Felicia said. "Can you?"

The color had drained from Shirley's cheeks, and her lips were trembling.

Mechanically, Felicia reached over and took the package. It was from a foreign country, she could tell by the postmark. And the heroin they were looking for was supposed to be smuggled from Turkey to France to America. At least, that was the normal route.

She looked at the package again. The stamps were

French! Her pulse hammered fiercely in the hollow of her throat, and her face was drawn taut. This could be it! This might be the package the men from the DEA had been waiting for.

"I think we had better call Miss Duncan," Felicia said.

At the mention of the dean of women, Miss McGuire drew herself erect. "And why should we bring Miss Duncan into this? The post office is my responsibility."

This was something Felicia hadn't reckoned on. In fact, now that she thought about it, she realized that they had thought of no course of action other than notifying Miss Duncan of anything suspicious.

"I thought she might know what we should do with it," Felicia murmured, "that's all."

"There is a course of procedure set down by the post office that is to be followed in such cases," Miss McGuire continued, her voice prim and impeccable. "We are to do what we can to determine the true owner of the parcel in question. If that can't be accomplished in a reasonable length of time, we are to return it to the central post office in Wellington for final disposition."

Shirley, who had said nothing until that moment, touched the package with a slender forefinger.

"That handwriting is familiar," she said aloud.

Felicia gasped, and a vague uneasiness swept over her, the chill wind of doubt.

"Are you positive?" Miss McGuire asked.

Shirley studied the package again. "In the last year, I've gotten half a dozen or more packages addressed in that handwriting. And, look, this was sent to my home address and readdressed to the school."

Felicia hadn't noticed that, but now that Shirley mentioned it, she realized that she was right about it.

"And," Shirley continued, "Dad is the one who readdressed it to me. I'd recognize his handwriting any place."

Miss McGuire frowned. "The postmark is from France," she reminded her.

Momentarily, the new student stared at the package. "That's where the others came from," she said numbly.

"You mean the other packages you were telling us about came from France too?"

"Where else? My boyfriend – I mean my *former* boyfriend – Pete Cameron, has an uncle who imports stuffed animals from all over the world. He knows that I'm wild about them, so he said he was going to send me one whenever he gets in something that was new or unusual."

"I see." It was obvious that Miss McGuire had not made up her mind whether to believe Shirley. "That is interesting, Shirley. But I'm afraid that we're going to have to have a bit more proof than that before we're able to turn the parcel over to you."

"I don't much care whether I get it or not now that

I've broken up with him," she said numbly. "If you want to send it to the main post office in Wellington, it's all right with me."

Felicia studied the new girl's face. There wasn't the slightest trace of anger or irritation. And that in itself was remarkable. Most girls, including Felicia, would have been disturbed by Miss McGuire's lack of trust. Shirley acted as though she expected it.

"On the contrary," Miss McGuire countered, "if the parcel belongs to you, we want you to have it. Do you have any proof that it's supposed to be yours?"

"I've got a letter from Mr. Pritchard up in my room," she began, "telling me that – No, I burned it when I burned all of Pete's letters."

"That is too bad."

"But I know what he said he was sending me," she continued. "He wrote that he had come across a little factory in France where they made the cuddliest poodles he had ever seen. He said he had asked them to send me a pink one. He thought I would like that."

That information seemed to almost convince Miss McGuire. "And you're saying this package has a pink poodle in it?"

"If it belongs to me, it does."

Miss McGuire fingered the corner of the green customs declaration slip that had not been torn off. "Perhaps we should refer this matter to Miss Duncan after all."

Miss Duncan came to the postal room in response

to Miss McGuire's call, her heels clacking an efficient beat on the terrazzo floor. She picked up the package, holding it thoughtfully.

"You say you've had other packages like this one, Miss Ellis," she began. "Did they come here to the school? And were the addresses torn off of them?"

"I've had two others since I started school here. I think they had been sent directly here though. I don't think Dad had to forward them."

"That's strange."

"I figure maybe Mr. Pritchard had lost my new address after he mailed the other packages."

"I suppose that's quite possible. But were they torn this way?"

"I don't believe they were. No, I don't think they were torn at all."

"Should I phone the postal inspector, Miss Duncan?" Miss McGuire asked hopefully.

The dean of women pursed her lips. "I doubt that it will be necessary at this point. I'm reasonably certain that we can handle the matter without bothering the postal people."

She weighed the package in her hand momentarily, her eyes sweeping the little group. "We'll open the package, Miss McGuire. If it is a pink poodle, it must belong to Shirley Ellis. If it should prove to be something else, it will have to become a matter for the regular post office."

Miss McGuire took the package back to a small

table, snipped the cord and unwrapped it as precisely as though she were unwrapping so many eggs. A thin strip of pink winked through at them.

"I was right!" Shirley said with delight. "It is the poodle!"

Shirley picked up the toy dog and held him tenderly, enjoying the softness in her hand.

"Does this mean I can keep him, Miss Duncan?" she asked.

The dean of women's smile winked. "I see no reason why you can't. It's obvious to me that the package belonged to you."

"Oh, thank you!" For an instant, it appeared that she might throw her arms around Miss Duncan and kiss her in appreciation. But the older woman pulled herself erect.

"A proper Wellington girl maintains control of her emotions at all times."

Shirley held the pink poodle up to her face, caressing him. "Isn't he precious? I just love him."

Felicia didn't know whether she was happy about the fact that the package contained the poodle or not. The way it worked out, Shirley had told the truth, and opening the package proved it. At least, it proved that she knew what was inside.

And the story about Pete's uncle importing toy animals was logical. Practically every store in the country had stuffed animals from Europe for sale. Someone had to import them. But Felicia's blood chilled when she thought about the heroin that was being smuggled in from France. It could be just a coincidence, but it scarcely seemed likely. The only logical explanation she could think of was that Shirley actually was involved in smuggling heroin.

And she couldn't square that with Shirley's new faith in Christ and her bitterness against drugs – unless her Christianity was a sham and her opposition to drugs an act to help mask her real purpose in being at Wellington. But Shirley seemed to be so honest, so open, and without deceit. It was impossible to believe that she could go through such an elaborate pretense for any purpose. Felicia's mind churned painfully.

As soon as they finished working, Shirley rewrapped the poodle hurriedly and started for her room with it.

"Want to come along, Felicia?"

Felicia and the new student started across the campus to their dormitory. Shirley was still chattering excitedly about the poodle she had just received in the mail when she stopped suddenly and grasped Felicia's arm with trembling fingers.

She spun quickly to stare at her friend. Shirley's cheeks were pale, and fear showed in her eyes.

"What's wrong, Shirley?" she whispered.

Her companion fought for composure. "Those men!" she exclaimed. "Who are they?"

Felicia shuddered. That could only mean one thing!

"Who are those men?" Shirley asked again, insistence honing her voice.

"They're just a couple of men who were in to see Miss Duncan about three weeks ago. Why? Do you know them?"

"I think I've seen them before," she answered lamely. "Or maybe they just look like someone I know."

Although Shirley tried to act as though any contact she had with Larramore and Miles had been casual and of no importance, she waited on the walk until the two men were inside the administration building. And when she started forward, all conversation was choked off. It was as though she had completely forgotten that Felicia was with her.

CHAPTER 11

A SEARCH WARRANT?

Miss Duncan ushered Larramore and Miles into her private office and closed the door behind them.

"I've been expecting you to check back with me," she said.

"We got tied up on something."

"That's right," Miles added. "There are some new developments on the heroin-smuggling case that we had to trace down. Just couldn't get back to you."

Miss Duncan replied, "If you hadn't come in today, I was going to call your office and ask them to have you get in touch with me."

"Did you have some reason for wanting to get in touch with us?"

The dean of women nodded. "I wanted to tell you that a package came in today for one of our students – a package from France."

"Ah!" His eyes gleamed.

"Are you sure it was from France?" Miles asked.

"It was from France, all right. A pink toy poodle that looks so lifelike you almost expect it to bark."

The lines around Larramore's mouth deepened. "A stuffed animal! That's a clever dodge."

"How did it get through, Larramore?" his companion wanted to know. "They're stopping everything for the school that goes through customs, aren't they?"

"They're supposed to. We'll have to ask a few questions of somebody." He whipped out his notebook.

"I think I can answer that for you," Miss Duncan said. The package was actually sent to the girl's home address and her parents forwarded it here."

"Hmm. That's clever."

Larramore acted as though he had more questions to ask, but Miles squirmed uncomfortably. "Hadn't we better be getting with it, Larramore?" he demanded. "Every minute that passes now gives them that much better chance to spirit it away."

The taller man frowned. "I suppose you're right. We can come back later and get more detailed information if we need it." He closed his briefcase and set it on his knee. "Now, if you'll give us the name of the girl who received the package and the master key to unlock her room, we'll be most grateful."

"Miss Shirley Ellis is the girl who received the package," Miss Duncan said quietly.

"Thank you." Larramore made a brief notation in

the slender black book he was carrying. "And now, if you'll give us the master key, we won't trouble you any further."

The dean of women frowned. "I'm sorry," she said, "but I can't do that. You'll have to have a search warrant before I can allow you to go through Miss Ellis's room."

"A search warrant?" Larramore said. "Do you realize how long that can take? The heroin can be on the West Coast or in Chicago by the time we could get back here with a search warrant."

Miss Duncan nodded almost imperceptibly. "I am aware of the problems getting a search warrant will cause, but it is something you will have to do if you want to search Miss Ellis's room. We must protect her rights."

"Even if she's involved in a dirty, rotten business like heroin smuggling?"

Miss Duncan nodded her agreement. "Even if she's involved in a dirty, rotten business like heroin smuggling. She's entitled to the protection of the law."

Miles leaned forward. "Are we to take that to mean that you refuse to cooperate with us?"

"You can take it any way you like. The breaking of one law doesn't give anyone the right to break another. If you would like to have me do it, I can call Miss Ellis in and request her permission to make the search. If she grants it, you will be at liberty to make your search."

Previously, only Miles had wanted to leave. Now, however, both men were anxious to be on their way. They got to their feet quickly, thanked Miss Duncan, and started out. They were in the outer office when Larramore turned around and went back for a final word with Miss Duncan.

"I'm going to have to insist that you keep this visit confidential," he told her guardedly. "One word to the wrong person and months of work would be lost."

Miss Duncan returned his gaze with her own cold, impersonal eyes. "Young man, as I told you before, I was practicing discretion when you were toddling around. You don't have to warn me of the importance of keeping quiet about a matter of this nature."

CHAPTER 12

ANOTHER PHONE CALL

Felicia was so disturbed by the events that day she could scarcely think of anything else. She felt that she had to find Joan and talk with her. With that in mind, she hurried back to the library as soon as she could get away from Shirley, but her friend wasn't there. When she did find her at the snack shop, she was with three others, so there was no chance of talking with her there. It was not until they were finally in their room that night after dinner that she had an opportunity to talk with her roommate about the things that had happened.

Joan was curious but found it difficult to believe that Shirley had actually been afraid of Larramore and Miles.

"It just doesn't sound like her," she countered. "She's not the sort to get frightened easily."

"Maybe not, but she was scared when she saw

them, I can tell you that. She was terribly scared. Her face was as gray as death."

Joan's eyes narrowed. "Come to think of it, she would be frightened if she suddenly became aware of the fact that the DEA was closing in on her."

Felicia nodded seriously. "There's got to be some reason for her to be as afraid as she was today when she saw them." She inhaled deeply. "I hate to admit it, but I'm beginning to believe that Shirley's *got* to be mixed up in this business."

"Are you *sure?*" Joan asked.

Felicia crossed the room uneasily and sat down. "Shirley sure did act strangely when she got that pink poodle."

Her roommate waited for her to continue.

"It's a cute little thing, I've got to admit, but it's not cute enough to rave over it the way she did. When I think about the fuss she made over it, I feel that she must have been trying to impress us about how excited she was over it and what it meant to her."

Joan's eyes gleamed. "I don't think it would mean that much to me either if it was just something cute to look at, as you said."

"And a stuffed animal could be an excellent place to hide drugs, for one thing."

"I suppose you're right," Joan said doubtfully, "but could they get enough heroin in a little animal like that to make it profitable?"

"I'm sure they could," Felicia replied. "I don't

have the slightest clue as to what it's worth, but I'm sure they could probably get twenty thousand dollars' worth of the awful stuff in a toy animal like the pink poodle."

Joan shuddered. "It gives me the cold chills just to think about it." The silence hung heavily in the room around them. "But the question is, what can we do about it? How are we going to find out if there's any heroin hidden in the pink poodle, I mean?"

Felicia drew herself erect, her blue eyes pensive. It was almost a minute later before she spoke. "If we could just get our hands on that poodle for thirty minutes without Shirley being around, we could find out whether there's any heroin in it or not."

Joan wasn't so sure that could be accomplished. "It might be all right if we could get the poodle for a while without having her peeking over our shoulders. But exactly how could we manage that? Shirley's going to guard that little stuffed poodle like it's made of gold until she's gotten rid of what's in it."

"You may be right," Felicia told her. "But we've got to try."

Joan stood once more, uneasily. "I suppose we could go to Miss Duncan about it. She'd probably be able to tell us what to do."

Felicia brushed her hand across her forehead. "We could go to her, but what could we tell her? We don't really know anything more than she does. She knows where the poodle came from, and she knows

Shirley has it." She paused for the space of a minute or more. "And, besides, if Shirley is innocent, I'd hate to cause her any more trouble than she's in already."

Joan's eyes widened. "I can't understand you, Felicia. After all the evidence against Shirley, you still insist that she could be innocent. I don't see how you can be so naive."

Felicia inhaled deeply. She hoped she wasn't being naive about Shirley. There had been times when she seriously doubted that Shirley could be innocent because of the stack of circumstantial evidence against her. Yet she knew that if she were in Shirley's position, she would want to be considered innocent until she had been proven guilty. There was a prayer in her heart as she went back to her studies, asking God to help her with the new student and to treat her the way a Christian should.

After a time, she closed her history book and looked up.

"Can you study tonight, Joan?"

"You ought to know better than to ask that. I always have trouble studying."

Felicia pushed herself away from her desk and got up. "Let's go down and see if Shirley's in her room. Maybe we can find out something by talking to her."

They went down the corridor to the room where Shirley and Karen lived, but neither of the girls was there.

"Maybe they had dates tonight," Joan suggested.

Felicia shook her head. "During the middle of the week? Are you out of your mind? If they did, they'd have to answer to Miss Duncan. It would probably be the end of both of them."

Her roommate shuddered. "What a horrible thought!"

"So, I guess the only thing we can do is to wait until morning to talk with her."

The following morning, Felicia and Joan did not sit at their usual places for breakfast. Instead, they sought out Shirley and Karen, who had gone to the far corner of the dining hall and were sitting with their heads close together, talking in low tones.

"Hi, we've been looking all over for you," Joan said, setting her tray on the table and pulling out a chair. "Is this a private argument, or can anyone get in on it?"

Shirley's smile winked on. "We were just talking about the phone call I had from Pete last night."

"That must have been where you were when we went down to your room to see you."

"That's where we were. After I talked with him, I was so upset that I got Karen to go out for a little walk with me. We weren't gone long."

"It was some conversation," Karen told them. "He talked for an hour trying to get her to take him back."

Felicia could not keep from frowning, and a question glittered in her eyes.

"You don't need to get so uptight about it, Felicia,"

Karen continued. "Shirley wouldn't budge. It was the most stupid thing I'd ever heard of. There she was crying her eyes out because she thinks so much of him, but she's not going to go out with him anymore."

"There's no use in our discussing it anymore, Karen," her roommate said quietly. "You simply don't understand."

"You can say that again." She shrugged helplessly. "I've been trying to talk some sense into Shirley's head ever since we got up this morning, but she's so freaked out over religion that she won't pay any attention to a thing I say." She glanced at Felicia and Joan, a wry grin tugging upward at the corners of her mouth. "And you two are as fanatical as she is, so I can't expect any help from you."

Joan's smile was warm and friendly, but instead of answering Karen, she directed her attention to Shirley. "I suppose Pete was upset because you don't want to go out with him anymore."

"Sort of."

"*Sort* of?" Karen echoed. "That's the understatement of the century. He said he got her letter and called to get things straightened out. At first, he practically bawled when he saw that his pleading wasn't going to get him anywhere with Shirley. Then he got mad and said that if that was the way things were, he wanted all the gifts he had ever given her returned."

"I really don't want them," Shirley said. "If they're

of any use to him, he can have them. All they do is remind me of him."

"I think I'd feel the same way," Felica said.

"I've even debated putting all the stuffed animals his uncle gave me in a box and giving them to him too. But I don't know whether I should or not."

"Tell her that you think she's ridiculous," Karen said. "Those animals never did belong to Pete. Why should he get them to give to some other girl? If you don't want them, give them to Felicia and Joan and me. We'll take them, won't we?"

With Karen at the table and in such a talkative mood, there was no chance for either Felicia or Joan to draw any information out of Shirley. They finished breakfast and excused themselves.

"I really should go back to our room and study," Joan said.

"You study? That's a switch."

"I said I *should*," she told them, laughing. "I didn't say that I was going to."

When they were gone, Karen turned back to her roommate seriously. "I know I am repeating myself, but I can't understand you at all. Giving up a handsome boyfriend like Pete Cameron because of religion just doesn't make sense."

Shirley fumbled for words. How could she find any different way of trying to tell Karen the reason for her decision. She was about to speak when her roommate continued talking, her voice scarcely above a whisper.

"I don't understand you, Shirley," she said. "In fact, I think you're nuts for doing what you did. But I do have to admit that I envy you."

Shirley's eyes widened. "What do you mean?"

Karen's manner softened, and wistfulness drove the scorn from her eyes. "It must be wonderful to have a purpose in life that means so much to you you'll give up a very special boyfriend because of it. I'd give anything to have purpose and direction like that for my life."

"You can," Shirley told her. "All you have to do is ask Jesus Christ to take away your sin and give you a new life."

Karen's face grew pensive. "I don't think so," she murmured. "I don't think I'd be willing to pay the price." With that, as though she was afraid to allow the conversation to continue, she pushed her chair back from the table and stood. "Sorry, Shirley, I've got to run."

Although Felicia and Joan thought about the new student and her boyfriend a great deal the rest of the day, they didn't see Shirley until after dinner that evening when she came to their room.

"I hope you don't mind my barging in on you this way," she said, "but I've got to have someone I can talk to."

"We're glad you came," Joan told her. "Sit down, won't you?"

Shirley settled uneasily into a chair. Silence dominated the room.

"I just had another phone call from Pete," she said at last, "and I couldn't talk to Karen. She won't try to understand."

Felicia and Joan nodded sympathetically.

"Is Pete still trying to get you to take him back?" Felicia wanted to know.

Shirley shook her head. "He's given up on that. Now he's decided that he wants me to give him back all the gifts that he gave me and all the gifts his uncle gave me. He told me to put them in a box and have it in the lounge downstairs so he can pick them up when he comes in tomorrow."

Felicia and Joan glanced quickly at each other. If that happened, they might never know whether there was heroin in the pink poodle or not.

"Are you going to do it?" Joan asked, trying not to sound too concerned about it.

"That's what I want to talk with you about." A new earnestness crept into her voice. "Do you think I ought to give him the stuffed animals his uncle gave me or not?"

Felicia thought a moment before speaking.

"Did Pete buy them from his uncle for you?" she asked after a time.

"Oh, no, nothing like that. I met his uncle when

he asked Pete if he knew of anyone who would type some letters for him. When I wouldn't take any money for it, he said he would send me some of his stuffed animal imports. So, actually, Pete had nothing to do with it."

"That's the way I would look at it," Felicia told her. "You worked for the gifts, so I see no reason why they ought to go to Pete."

"That's how I see it too," Joan broke in. "If I were you and wanted to keep them, I certainly would."

Shirley talked with Felicia and Joan for a few minutes and had a cup of tea with them. When she finally got up to go, she said impulsively, "Thank you so very much. You'll never know how much help you've been to me tonight. I'm going to give him all of the gifts he gave me, but I've decided to keep the other things."

Felicia closed the door behind her and turned slowly, her gaze seeking Joan's. "What do you think of that?"

"I don't know for sure, but it sounds to me as though we're not the only ones who are anxious to get their hands on that pink poodle."

"That's just what I was thinking. Somehow, we've got to get hold of that poodle."

"But how? That's going to be the problem." Joan went over to her desk and sat down thoughtfully. "Maybe it's too late now. Maybe the heroin or whatever came in the stuffed animal is already gone."

"No," Felicia said, shaking her head. "It isn't gone, or Shirley's old boyfriend wouldn't be trying to get hold of it."

Joan turned to face her. "Aren't we getting ahead of ourselves?" she asked. "We're assuming that he's one of the smugglers just because he wants to get those animals away from Shirley."

"That was the only reason I could think of for his wanting them."

"Maybe," Joan replied, "and maybe not. He could be so mad at Shirley that he wants to get back at her for refusing to date him anymore. Did you ever think of that?"

Felicia's smile was thin and humorless. "I guess you're right. I was just trying to find some reason to believe that Shirley's innocent, that's all. I guess I was trying to build up some sort of a case against her old boyfriend in my mind."

The clock struck somberly, and they waited until it had finished before either spoke again.

"Just the same, we've got to get that pink poodle long enough to find out if there's something in it!" Felicia said, determination firming her voice.

CHAPTER 13

A SCREAM IN THE NIGHT!

The next afternoon when Felicia and Joan saw Shirley, they were surprised by the change that had come over her. Her eyes were dancing, and a bright, vivacious smile lighted her attractive young face.

"What happened to you?" Joan asked impulsively. "You look as though you inherited a million dollars."

"I did – more or less." She lowered her voice. "Pete called me a little while ago, and I told him he could have every gift he had given me but that I'm going to keep the things his uncle gave to me."

"What did he say to that?" Felicia wanted to know.

"He got mad," she said, giggling, "and told me to keep everything if I was going to be that way."

"You don't act as though you feel very bad about it."

"I'm glad that it's finally over. You know, when he was talking so terribly to me, I was so glad I had broken up with him. It was just as though someone had pulled back a curtain to let me see what he's really like."

The three of them walked down the corridor together.

"I'm not going to keep his gifts, of course," she continued. "I'll mail them back to him in a few days. And I might even send back the things his uncle gave me. They really don't mean that much to me. But I'm going to wait until he knows he didn't frighten me with all those threats of what he was going to do if he didn't get those things returned by tomorrow." She paused uneasily, as though the full import of Pete's threats was just pushing into awareness.

"But there's something I can't quite figure out," she murmured. "Pete acted as though he was a lot more anxious to get his hands on the things his uncle gave me than on anything that he had given me himself. It's awfully strange."

Felicia eyed her questioningly but remained silent. When Shirley talked that way, she couldn't help being convinced that she had nothing whatever to do with any heroin smuggling. She was so open and unaffected, so natural in the things she said and did.

She couldn't help thinking, however, that there was something unusual about Pete's interest in the collection of stuffed animals his uncle had given to Shirley unless it was the way Karen said that he was determined to get them away from her as spite for turning him down.

She didn't know how she and Joan were going to do it, but they were going to have to get their hands on that pink poodle and soon – before it was too late.

That night, Felicia went to bed at the usual time, but she had difficulty sleeping. Her mind kept churning over the whole matter of the heroin smuggling and Shirley and Larramore and Miles and Pete Cameron. At last, from sheer exhaustion, she began to drift off into unconsciousness but only to dream. She could see Shirley's pretty, young face staring at her and the new pink poodle she held in her arms. Felicia could feel herself reaching out for the stuffed animal as she wavered in that vague land between consciousness and sleep. The poodle seemed to come alive as she reached for him, and he backed up, stiffly, always keeping just beyond her fingertips.

She was trying to grasp the poodle in her dream when a wild, terrified scream blasted her awake. She jerked upright, trembling violently.

"What was that?" Joan cried. "What happened?"

"I don't know!" Felicia leaped out of bed and scrambled into her robe. "But there's something terribly wrong!"

Joan was half a step behind her. When they pushed out into the hall, other girls were popping out of their rooms, faces white and lifeless and eyes stark with fear.

"What's happened, Felicia?" someone asked, her voice quavering.

She shook her head. All she actually knew was that there had been a wild, piercing scream from down the hall. "It sounded as though it came from this direction. It must be from Shirley's room!"

Felicia and Joan pushed down the corridor frantically to their friend's door, followed by the other girls.

"Shirley!" Felicia shouted. "Shirley! Are you and Karen all right?"

A moment later, the door opened, revealing two terrified girls.

"What is it? What's wrong?"

Karen was the one who spoke, the words tumbling from her quavering lips. "There–there was a man in our room! He came through the fire escape and–and–Oh, it was horrible!"

"Did he hurt you?"

She acted as though she hadn't even heard what Joan asked her. "He–he just stood there with that mask over his face and told us to be quiet if we didn't want to get hurt. But we couldn't help screaming, and he cursed us and ran away!"

Just then the dormitory supervisor came hurrying up. "What was that scream?" Miss Miller asked. "What's wrong? Has someone been hurt?"

Shirley told her what had just taken place. Miss Miller's concern was evident. "Are you both all right? He didn't harm either of you, did he?"

"Yes, we're all right," Karen said. "He came in the fire escape and was standing right in our room not a yard from our beds! I woke up and–and there he was!" She shuddered just remembering what had happened.

Miss Miller went into the room Shirley and Karen shared. She flinched slightly as she saw that the window was open, and there was a big, wet footprint on the carpet just below it.

"Was anything stolen?" she wanted to know.

The girls eyed each other questioningly.

"We don't know," Shirley answered. "We've been too frightened to look."

Miss Miller took firm command of the situation. "Felicia, please call Miss Duncan and tell her what has happened. I will stay here with Karen and Shirley and try to determine whether anything has been stolen. The rest of you go back to your rooms and get some rest. There will be classes as usual in the morning."

"But Miss Miller!" one of the girls protested. "We can't go to our rooms and go to sleep now. Not after what happened!"

"You have nothing to fear," she said crisply. "I am here and will remain until the police arrive to check the grounds."

The police came in response to Miss Duncan's call, arriving shortly after she did. They checked the grounds and the buildings thoroughly and questioned Shirley and Karen at length.

There was little more the girls could tell them

beyond the fact that they had gone through their belongings and could find nothing missing.

"You won't have to worry anymore," the officer in charge said. "Enough men will be assigned to guard duty here to give complete protection for everyone."

"We have our own security guards," Miss Duncan informed him, "but I will appreciate it if your men will keep a close watch on the dormitory until this character is caught. You know how dangerous that sort can be."

The officer asked a few more questions and glanced at his notebook. "We may ask you girls to come down to the station in a day or two and look through some mugshots to see if we can get a line on our man. But, in the meantime, don't worry about the guy getting back in again. We will assign a couple of men to the school for a few nights to assist your own security guard."

No one in the dorm slept any more that night. And, shortly after six o'clock the next morning, Shirley came to Felicia and Joan's room, carrying a double armload of stuffed animals.

"I hated to come so early," she said, "but I wanted to get them down here before any of the other girls were out in the hall to see me."

Felicia and Joan eyed her curiously but asked no questions. Shirley dumped her load of animals on the rug beside Joan's bed.

"Would you hide them here in your room for me for a while?" she asked guardedly.

"Of course, we will. But why? Are you afraid someone will steal them?"

A sheepish grin tugged at the corners of Shirley's mouth. "I suppose it sounds silly, but after the police and everybody left last night, I got to thinking about what had happened, and I keep coming back to these toy animals. It seems to me that they've got to have something to do with that man breaking into our room last night."

"But why?"

"I don't know for sure," Shirley went on. "Maybe it was because of some of the wild things that Pete said when he called yesterday morning and I told him I wasn't going to give him the gifts his uncle had given to me. He talked as though they were something more than cute little animals to put on my bed and around our room. I didn't say anything to anyone about it because I couldn't figure it out. I still can't. But I don't want to have them stolen, so I decided to bring them here."

"Did you ever try to find out if they're valuable?" Joan asked her.

"I've poked around in them to see if they might have something hidden in them, if that's what you mean. But I couldn't find a thing."

The girls discussed several hiding places with her and finally decided on putting them under the bed.

"I've heard that the best place to hide things is often in a very obvious place," Felicia said.

"Besides," Joan added, "whoever looks under *our* beds? The girls all know we never clean under them. It's the perfect hiding place."

As soon as Shirley was gone, the girls both dove for the pink poodle, jerking it hurriedly from under the bed.

"We've got it!" Joan whispered triumphantly. "We've got it!"

Felicia found an old razor blade she kept in her sewing kit and a spool of pink thread that was very close to the color of the poodle.

"Help me hold him, Joan. We've got to work fast if we're going to get this done before time for breakfast."

Cutting the seam was only the work of a minute. Then Felicia began to pull out the downy stuffing.

"Have you found anything?" Joan asked curiously.

She shook her head.

At that moment, there was the swift sound of shoes in the hall outside, their door was flung open suddenly, and Shirley burst in.

"I found–" Her voice choked off in midsentence.

CHAPTER 14

SUCCESSFUL OPERATION

Felicia and Joan flushed scarlet under Shirley's astonished eyes.

"What are you doing?" she demanded incredulously.

They looked at each other and then at the girl who had just come into their room, as embarrassed as they had ever been in their lives.

"I guess we had the same idea you did," Felicia stammered. "We were looking to see if something had been smuggled into the country in your toy dog."

Shirley reached down and touched the half-stuffed poodle with the tip of her finger.

"I can't say that I blame you," she said, suddenly numb. "It seems that strange things have been going on ever since I got here." She inhaled deeply. "I thought those things just happened – Larramore and Miles coming to see Miss Duncan and everything."

"Did you know them?" Joan broke in.

"I know that they're narcotics men." Her throat constricted tightly, and it was a minute or more before she could go on. Both girls waited patiently. "Then, when I talked with Pete yesterday and he was so angry about those stuffed animals, I figured they had to have something to do with drug smuggling. That was the only thing it could be."

Shirley picked up the poodle, smiling crookedly. "I can tell you right now that you're wasting your time on this little project. I already split him open and had a look at his insides, but there wasn't anything there but stuffing."

Felicia's spirits soared. This meant that Shirley hadn't been mixed up in heroin smuggling. It meant that her Christian testimony and her efforts to help other kids see the dangers of drugs were both genuine.

There were times when she and Joan had doubted Shirley's innocence, she had to admit that. But she was glad that she had stayed by her and that neither she nor Joan had turned against her or hindered her in any way. Knowing that Shirley wasn't guilty was like lifting a terrible weight from her shoulders. Felicia sighed and thanked God for Shirley and her firm faith in Him.

"Do you think your former boyfriend is involved in this mess?" Joan wanted to know.

"I'd hate to think he was," Shirley replied as honestly as she knew how. "But he used to act very strange at times." She shifted her poodle from one arm to the other and brushed a hand nervously through her hair. "And especially the way he acted when I talked with him on the phone yesterday morning."

Felicia straightened slowly, a faraway look in her eyes. "If the pink poodle is a part of this heroin smuggling act, Pete's uncle would have to be in on it too."

Shirley frowned. "I'd never thought of that." She took a deep breath. "But you're right. He would have to be." There was a long, pained silence. "I just thought of something. If Pete and his uncle are in on this thing together, the chances are that Pete only dated me because he wanted to use me." Hurt laced her eyes.

"I don't think that follows, necessarily," Felicia said. "After you were a Christian and came here to Wellington, he could have decided you would be a good tool to use in their smuggling racket."

Shirley's smile was soft and friendly. "Thanks for that, Felicia. It isn't very flattering to think that a boy would go out with you only because he wanted to use you as a means of doing something illegal."

"I hate to break up this little love fest," Joan blurted, "but we're going to have to go down to breakfast in a few minutes, and we're no closer to making anything out of this riddle than we were before."

"Maybe a good breakfast will be just what we need to help us think better," Shirley said.

Felicia finished pushing the last bit of stuffing into the pink poodle, patted and poked it into place so he had no unseemly bumps, and started to sew up the seam once more.

Joan looked at her watch.

"If we're going to have that breakfast we've been talking about, we'd better get with it," she said. "You know, a Wellington girl is always prompt, and, in an effort to encourage promptness, meals at the school are only served at specified times."

"You sound just like Miss Duncan," Shirley giggled.

"I should. I've heard her repeat the rules and regulations of this place often enough."

Felicia held the pink poodle momentarily, then lifted one corner of the spread and shoved him under the bed with the rest of the stuffed animals.

"Do you think it's safe there?" Joan asked.

"It ought to be safe enough. Nobody else knows that it's in here."

"We hope."

They left the dormitory, hurrying across the campus in the chill March breeze, still concerned about the pink poodle and the part it played in the heroin smuggling operation.

"I can't figure it out," Felicia said again. "We've gone over that little animal with everything except a magnifying glass, and there's not a sign of any heroin or anything else except stuffed poodle."

"Maybe there isn't anything else," Joan said. "Did you ever think of that?"

"But there's got to be!" Felicia retorted. "If there

isn't, none of the things that have happened make sense. That poodle has to have a part in this heroin smuggling business."

They were sitting in the dining hall eating breakfast when Shirley mentioned going to see Miss Duncan. "I think we ought to see her and tell her everything. She might be able to help us."

Felicia nodded. "I think that's an excellent idea."

"So do I," Joan added, "in spite of all the opportunities I get to see her."

As soon as they finished breakfast, they hurried to the administration building and went directly to Miss Duncan's office. Usually, she was working by that time, her glasses settled firmly on the bridge of her nose, but that morning, her office door was closed and locked.

"It doesn't look as though anyone's here."

At that moment, Miss Hanson came hurrying up, puffing breathlessly. "I'm sorry, girls, but I had some errands to do for Miss Duncan this morning on the way down. She won't be in today, you know."

Disappointment clouded Shirley's eyes. "You mean she won't be here at all today?"

Miss Hanson unlocked her office, switched on the light, and took off her coat, still harried and a bit upset.

"Now, what was it you wanted to know?"

"Will Miss Duncan be in at all today?" Shirley repeated.

Miss Hanson glanced at the appointment calendar. "I'm sure she won't be here before 3:00, if she comes at all, and it may be as late as 5:00 or 5:30." She eyed them curiously. "Is there something I can do for you?"

"Oh, no," Shirley said quickly. "No, thank you."

"If she does come in this afternoon, I can have her call you if you'd like."

The girls asked her to tell Miss Duncan they had been in to see her and that they would stay in their rooms until dinner at 6:30 so she could get them if she wanted to call them, thanked her, and went outside.

"I guess that's one idea that didn't amount to much," Shirley said.

"It might amount to more than we think right now," Joan answered. "If Miss Duncan gets back today, she'll call us. You can be sure of that."

The rest of the day moved endlessly for Felicia and her friends. They had a surprise quiz in English Lit. that afternoon, and Felicia was sure that she had gotten a poor grade. She couldn't concentrate when all she could think of was Shirley and Larramore and Miles and the pink poodle her boyfriend wanted so badly. At last, the school day limped to a close.

The girls went over to the administration building to see if Miss Duncan had gotten back yet, but she wasn't there.

"And I really don't know for sure when she will be coming in," Miss Hanson said as apologetically as though she had been responsible for Miss Duncan's absence.

"That's all right," Felicia said. "We'll wait for her in our room."

On the way over to the dormitory, Felicia paused, glancing at her companions. "You know, the more I think about that pink poodle, the more anxious I am to take another good look at it."

"What is it this time?" Joan wanted to know.

"I'm not sure." She was speaking hesitantly now, as though she wasn't even sure she wanted her companions to hear what she had in mind. "I'm not sure at all. But I've got the vague feeling that there's something wrong with that poodle – something we should have seen."

"I don't know what it could be," Joan said, "but I know you, Felicia. I know you're not going to be satisfied until you've taken that poor little stuffed animal apart again."

It did seem foolish to rip the stuffed poodle apart again after it had already been taken apart twice. She probably wouldn't find anything there. When she thought about it sensibly, she did have to admit that she had done everything she could already to find any drugs hidden in it. There couldn't be anything in it, that was for sure. And yet, that nagging uneasiness persisted as though there were something hiding just behind the curtain of her mind with only its toes sticking out to betray its presence.

Once in the room with the door locked, Felicia got out the pink poodle and picked up the razor blade again while Joan and Shirley crowded close, staring at her.

"I'm glad I didn't get finished," she said. "I'd just have that much more work to do."

"My poor little poodle," Shirley murmured. "I wonder if he'll ever be the same again."

While they were talking, Felicia slit the seam, and, turning a portion of the stuffed animal inside out, had Shirley and Joan feel the thickness of the material.

"Isn't it strange to use material as thick as this for a little stuffed animal?" she asked.

Joan rubbed it thoughtfully between her thumb and forefinger. "It is thick," she agreed, "and it's lined. Isn't that strange?"

Felicia nodded. "It's awfully strange to me." With that, she slit the lining a quarter of an inch or so, taking care to go through the lining.

Joan gasped. "Why, there is something in there, after all!"

The three girls stared at the slit in the fabric and the section of plastic bag filled with some sort of white powder that was exposed.

Shirley's face was ashen. "That's heroin!" she said, a hoarse, rasping tone in her voice. "It has to be!"

"Now I know what it was that disturbed me about the poodle," Felicia told them. "The material seemed so thick as I pulled it together to resew it. I remember thinking at the time that it was far heavier than it would have to be. But then I realized it was imported and thought maybe that was just the way they do it in France."

"It's the way they do it in France, all right," Joan said. "They've made a plastic bag a quarter of an inch thick or so on the pattern of the poodle, only a little smaller. Then they sewed a lining in it to cover the plastic filled with heroin."

Shirley was trembling violently, and her face was ashen. "So, that's why Pete was so anxious to get it back," she murmured.

The girls were standing there staring at each other when the phone rang in the corridor. A moment later, someone knocked on the door.

"Felicia and Joan, Miss Hanson just called and said that Miss Duncan will be in her office for another half an hour and will be waiting for you."

At the door, Shirley hesitated. "I know I've got to go and tell her what we know, but I feel almost like a traitor to Pete."

Felicia picked up the poodle, and the three girls left the room and went down the stairs and out into the spreading dusk.

"He's the one who ought to feel like a traitor to you," Felicia reminded her. "You dated him and thought he cared for you, but all the time he was going out with you so he could use you as a drop for getting heroin into the country."

In the growing dusk, the girls didn't even see the man until he was almost upon them, and then they didn't pay much attention to him. He approached them briskly, hat pulled low over his face and his coat collar yanked high to all but meet it.

When he was even with the girls, he turned suddenly and snatched at the pink poodle in Felicia's arms.

"No, you don't!" She tightened her grip on it and jerked back.

He swore and would have wrenched it from her hands in spite of her efforts to keep it, but Joan kicked him sharply on the shins. He yelped with pain and relaxed his hold on the pink poodle for an instant.

That was all Felicia needed! She sped away, tucking the poodle in her arms and screaming lustily. Shirley and Joan were also screaming as loudly as two healthy young ladies could scream.

The man tried desperately to get away, but he was doomed before he had moved a dozen yards. The school security guard swarmed in and grabbed him while he was still on campus.

Shirley was crying quietly.

"Don't be so upset," Felicia tried to comfort her. "It's all over now. Everyone will know that you didn't have anything to do with what happened."

She looked up. "It was Pete," she choked. "It was Pete."

Felicia put an arm around her but said no more. This was not a time for words.

CHAPTER 15

A NEW JOY

Karen was waiting anxiously for Shirley and Felicia and Joan to come back from Miss Duncan's office where they gave depositions to Larramore and Miles.

"Oh, I was so frightened when I heard what happened," she exclaimed. "Did they get all of them?"

"Mr. Larramore said that they would make the final arrest before morning."

"What I can't figure out is why it was so important to stop a smuggled shipment like this one in the stuffed animal," Karen went on. "Surely they couldn't get more than a few ounces in each one."

"That's right," Felicia answered, "but you want to remember that Shirley had received nine stuffed animals already. Think of the amount of heroin that could be smuggled into the country a few ounces at a time."

"That's right," Joan said. "Eventually, they could

have sent in several million dollars' worth of heroin, and probably no one would have been the wiser."

"And," Shirley broke in, "you've got to remember that a few ounces of heroin is worth a tremendous amount of money."

"There's something I still don't understand, Shirley," Felicia said. "I can see how they got the heroin in, all right, but how did they get it after you received the stuffed animal?"

"I've been thinking about that too. Then I remembered that after I got each new animal from Pete's uncle, Pete would ask to borrow it for a week. He said that he showed it to salesmen, and his uncle gave him a commission on each order he took."

Felicia's eyes gleamed. "So, he would take the animals, open them up, and get out the heroin. Then he'd have them restuffed to bring back to you."

"That's the only explanation I can figure out."

"It sounds logical to me."

"It sounds logical to me too," Joan put in. "And I'm glad that it's over."

"So am I," Shirley added.

Karen's gaze found hers. "I was so sorry for you when I heard that Pete had been arrested. I know how terrible you must feel."

"I do feel bad," she admitted, "but not nearly the way I'd have felt if I hadn't broken up with him. If it hadn't been for my faith in Christ, the chances are that I'd never have broken up with him, and I might be in jail right now myself."

Karen's cheeks blanched. "I'd never thought of that."

After a time, Felicia and her roommate went back to their room, leaving Karen and Shirley alone.

"I thought they'd never go," Karen murmured.

"I thought you liked Felicia and Joan," Shirley said. "They've certainly been loyal friends to me."

"I do like them, but I wanted to talk to you alone." She squirmed nervously on her chair. "I owe you an apology. You did the right thing when you broke up with Pete. It would have been tragic for you if you hadn't."

"Of course, not every case is as plain as this one," Shirley reminded her, "but it's still best for a believer not to date a nonbeliever, just the same."

The silence was taut between them.

"You've shown me that you've got something I haven't got, Shirley," she said wistfully.

"You can have Christ too," the other girl told her. "All you have to do is to confess your sin and put your trust in Jesus Christ. It's very simple."

Their eyes met. "Will you pray with me?"

"Of course, I will."

Together, they knelt by Karen's bed, and she began to pray hesitantly, calling on Christ for the first time in all her life. The pain in Shirley's heart at Pete's betrayal was already gone, replaced by the joy of being able to help someone else find Christ as her Savior.

THE
FELICIA CARTRIGHT
SERIES

Felicia Cartright, a petite blonde who is one of the most popular students at Wellington School for Girls, has a surprising inclination toward mysteries. If a mysterious situation arises, it either makes its way to Felicia, or Felicia somehow finds it. Though this is a bit trying for her happy-go-lucky roommate, Joan Bailey, it does prevent life from becoming monotonous. It also enables Bernard Palmer, the popular author of the "Danny Orlis" books, to write an entertaining series of stories for girls aged twelve to eighteen.

The mysteries range from a valuable missing antique to an attempt by claim jumpers to steal a deposit of tungsten ore. There's excitement and action galore—but there's also spiritual guidance and blessing because Felicia and her partner-in-adventure love the Lord and take Him into account in all their experiences.